The Girl's Best Friend

A Collection of Essays on Love, Life, & Sharing Your Light

NATHAN HALE WILLIAMS

© 2017 Nathan Hale Williams
All rights reserved.

ISBN: 0692971963
ISBN 13: 9780692971963
Library of Congress Control Number: 2017917323
WHyN Press, Los Angeles, CA

For Andrea, Danielle, La, Brandi & Raquel
&
All of my best girlfriends!!! I love you all so much!

PLAYLIST

1. <u>The Greatest Love of All</u>—Self-Love/Self-Care   1
2. <u>Single Ladies</u>—Dating   69
3. <u>Spend My Life</u>—Marriage   163
4. <u>We Are Family</u>—Family & Friends   209
5. <u>I Look to You</u>—Spirit   265

FOREWORD
Excellence, Love, Gratitude…
All with a Tone of Fun

By Andrea J. Hargrave
COO, iN-Hale Entertainment (Lifelong BFF)

There are very few people born in the 1970s for whom the following statement is true: I have known Nathan Hale Williams for my entire life. I am blessed to be one of those few. You see, Nathan and I were raised together in the same church, and our birthdays are one month apart. (This is where he always inserts that mine is first!) So basically, there is not a point in time where I have done something without Nathan nearby, which is one of the keys to my success in life.

As children we were equally supportive of each other and competitive with each other. I remember things like the Dr. Martin Luther King Jr. program at church, where there was an essay competition and opportunities to perform in front of the church. We were fierce competitors—we each knew the other was going to bring something powerful and made sure to match it with a work of equal excellence. By the time the program was announced each year, we were either tied for first or presenting two different types of tributes. It helped that, as we evolved, our talents were more complementary, and we would often both be presented on the program: Nathan doing a reading and me at the piano. But the keyword in this paragraph is *excellence*.

In all things he does, Nathan strives for excellence. He only surrounds himself with those whom he sees demonstrating the same commitment to excellence. Nathan is amazingly discriminating with the people he spends significant amounts of time on or energy with. This is one of the things that makes him "The Girl's Best Friend." Nathan's energy motivates you to remain—or become—your highest version of yourself. Whenever I'm not channeling my best me, Nathan can immediately pick up on it and helps me figure out what's caused the shift within. When it's something like a major life event, he is the first to be supportive of giving time and space to mourn, be confused, behave unusually, or whatever is needed to start processing it. But when it's time to move on, he's the first to tell you to snap back to reality and pull yourself together. He'll help support you and push you along, but you've got to take that first step. And that's what best friends do. You're your natural best in their presence, they build a fence around you when you're not at your best, and they do everything humanly possible to bolster you toward your next level of achievement.

The moment I realized Nathan was my absolute best friend was a bit different from what most people experience. During our tween and teen years, Nathan and I "went together." As in boyfriend and girlfriend. Homecomings, proms, most special occasions in those years—we were an item. Our parents were pretty set that we would get married after college. Nathan had decided to become a neurosurgeon and would support my career as a classical pianist. We would have two children, live in Los Angeles with our dog…this was all pretty clear by the time we were about fifteen. After all, we already did just about everything together except go to the same school, and we couldn't wait to spend every day of the rest of our lives together. Until…I met a man. Who took my breath away differently from the way I felt with Nathan. Who made things tingle that hadn't been stimulated before. And as that relationship progressed, I realized I had to confront the proverbial elephant in the room. So, I called Nathan and had him come visit me in college. (I was still his girlfriend, after all!) This was back in the days when you could greet someone at the gate at the airport. I ran up to him, hugged him as hard as I possibly could, and then held hands and looked him directly in the eyes intently. I told him that we couldn't be boyfriend and girlfriend anymore, as I'd found someone I wanted to be in a serious relationship with. I also assured him that we would always be best friends. Not your run of the mill best friends we would be the absolute *best* of friends. And finally, I told him that I had someone for him to meet (which absolutely blew him away and turned out to be beyond hilarious!).

I tell that story because it was a turning point in our relationship. It was the moment that there was no awkward expectation or need to confront sex between Nathan and me. Which creates such a different dynamic in relationships between two genders. What had the potential to be devastating was completely freeing, because I realized the treasure of our relationship. I would share just about every moment for the rest of my life with this man as I had for my entire life beforehand. We talk about all things, from politics to relationships to pop culture to pageants to football. We cuddle. We laugh. We cry. We act silly. We play games with my two kids who are his Godchildren. We excel in business meetings. See, the gift in having "The Girl's Best Friend" as your actual best friend is having all of the discussions and advice, but with platonic intimacy too. Being able to share all of the scary and awkward things about yourself—and dish about every possible thing (including maybe getting some helpful sex tips here and there)—is *amazing*. And I can guarantee you that there is no better BFF in the game than Nathan Hale Williams. Trust me. I have seven older brothers *and* Nathan as my BFF. I know men. I know what I'm talking about. Nathan comes from a place of love, so even when the tone is stern, you know the root of it is love.

I've had quite a set of challenging situations and experiences in my life bundled with an abundance of blessings. Through it all, Nathan has been by my side (or in front, or behind pushing, wherever he needed to be). I am grateful for the depth and breadth of this relationship. Always starting from and going back to gratefulness is something I've adopted from him, and it continues to steer my attitude toward positivity and light. So, despite my Nathan selfishness (others call it my diva tendencies, but we don't listen to those people), I am pleased to share him with you through this book. Enjoy these pages, and know that I am grateful for all of the ways that my life is better because he is in my life. I look forward to seeing (on social media, of course!) how your life and outlook have been improved by his words and stories. World, I gift to you, *my* best friend, "The Girl's Best Friend," Nathan Hale Williams.

INTRODUCTION

I have a little secret to tell you. You have to promise to keep it to yourself. OK! Here goes. The term "relationship expert" scares me. I cringe a bit every time anyone uses the term to describe me. Sure, I wrote a relationship advice column for nearly five years for *Essence* magazine, and I have been giving relationship advice for over twenty years both formally and informally. But a relationship expert? That's a lot of pressure.

My relationships are far from perfect, and I don't propose to know it all. I remember, when the digital editor, Emil Wilbekin, first asked me to write "The Girl's Best Friend" column for *Essence* to talk about my experiences with my fabulous female friends, I was super excited. Then I had to write my first column, and I was terrified. I wasn't sure what I wanted to say or if anything I had to say was valuable. Turns out, once I overcame my initial apprehension, I had a lot to say, and many people found it valuable.

I think the thing that people appreciated the most was that my advice comes from a personal space. These were anecdotes and stories about my real friends and life. And I started from the position that there's nothing wrong with any of us. We all can continue to learn as life progresses; however, we are perfectly situated right where we are on our journey. So, I never took the position that it was my job to fix anyone, especially the women that read my column and *Essence* magazine. From what I have read, it seems that some of the men giving relationship advice to women don't really like women (based on the tone and tenor of the advice). As my first column stated, I love women, and I wanted that love to shine.

Another secret. Although I write from the perspective of my "sister-friends," many of my columns were about my male friends, and a lot more were about me. Since I was writing for *Essence*, I had to write from a female perspective. However, my columns are universal in origin and application. It was merely good advice that I have learned from listening, watching, and reading. Common sense living.

This book is a collection of my most popular as well as my favorite columns. It is designed to be read chronologically or out of order as needed—like a cookbook. Aside from some nips and tucks here and there, I resisted my burning desire to rewrite the columns. The good news is that, although some were written years ago, the advice still holds true. Now, I have updated references to ages/time; made notes about television, music, and movies that are from the past; and chopped any references to friends who are no longer friends (no shade…maybe a little). But all in all, this is what was published on Essence.com.

Along the way I have included little notes from my favorite girls about…*me*! Smile. It's more an exercise of professional reference than one of vanity. I want you to know that I earned the title, "The Girl's Best Friend" the good, old-fashioned way. By having amazing relationships with an amazing group of women. I posed some questions to them, and they were free to answer in whichever way they chose. I hope you enjoy the columns/essays. Please just don't call me a relationship expert. Cheers!

PROLOGUE

"Why I'm Every Girl's Best Friend"
From *Essence*.com, December 2010 (edited)

I love black women! Particularly, I love strong, intelligent, and loving black women. I guess you can say that I get it from my mother, the epitome of all of those wonderful, albeit somewhat cliché, adjectives. The truth can become cliché at times, but the truth it remains.

My television show *Leading Women* (formerly *Real Life Divas*) tells the triumphs and adversities of famous African-American women such as Dr. Maya Angelou, Susan Taylor, Iman, Congresswoman Maxine Waters, Jill Scott, and Yolanda Adams, to name a few. In too many instances, mainstream media overlooks the women profiled on my show, despite their numerous accomplishments, global contributions, and rich stories. As a people we know that we must celebrate us for us, which is why *Essence* remains necessary even as we assimilate and acculturate more into white society and culture. And yes, even when we have a black president.

My love for my mother, my grandmothers, my aunts, and my cousins translated into a love for my sisters. "Sisters" does not refer to my biological sisters—I'm an only child—nor does it reference the colloquial "my sistas" attached to women of African descent. For me, the term *sisters* refers to the women in my life who have, over time and experience, turned our friendships into relationships thicker than blood and deeper than mere ancestry; as Dr. Angelou says, these are my "sister-friends."

I have been fortunate to build a bond with some of the fiercest and baddest women out there. They are truly my family—my sisters—and they are diverse in every way possible. Some I've known for forty-one years. Others for a year. Some are housewives. Some are corporate moguls. Others are artists and comedians. Whatever their titles are, they all share one thing (besides me), and that is their commitment to being excellent: mothers, daughters, sisters, wives, girlfriends, and lovers.

Now, I don't want you to get the impression that I'm that guy that only hangs around women. I don't. I have great and lasting relationships with my boys—my brother-friends. As black men, we all too often get the short end of the stick. And I am really worried about our young boys and their future. But that's another column for another magazine. With that said, it is my unique position as a black gay man who has great relationships with straight men as well as straight women that finds me always being asked for advice from my sister-friends about guys.

Now, I'm not Steve Harvey or the other guys that try to tell you what to do or what you're doing wrong. Nor will you get any fashion or makeup tips from me. My perspective, however, has helped my sister-friends succeed in their relationships and in life, regardless of their titles, socioeconomic, or relationship statuses. Many of the topics will be humorous, with salacious-seeming titles, all the while giving you a little spirit and a lot of hope. So, my goal here is not to reinvent the Bible, but to offer a point of view that may help you too.

Hopefully you will laugh and maybe even be able to apply something to your life. Most importantly it's about celebrating my strong, intelligent, and loving black women. It's about celebrating *you*!

THE GREATEST LOVE OF ALL—SELF-LOVE/SELF-CARE

"So, I learned to depend on me."

—Linda Creed

"If you don't love yourself, how in the hell you gonna love somebody else?"

—RuPaul

FALL IN LOVE WITH YOU AGAIN

Writing this column from Venice, Italy, adds so many more levels of inspiration and introspection. Truly this is a place with a charm unaffected by time and a magic that beckons for your spirit to come alive. One of my friends said, "You will fall in love in Venice!" And I did. I fell in love with myself again.

For the past year, I've had to navigate some difficult moments with relationships. Naturally I pride myself on my ability to maintain and manage my relationships, hence why I'm able to write this column. With that said, I have found post-long-term-relationship dating difficult, and I have had to deal with the ending of a professional partnership and friendship.

My long-term relationship ended approximately two and a half years ago. Initially I found the freedom of single life to be exciting and a breath of fresh air. Recently, like many other single people, I have found dating to be exhausting and the pickings to be very slim. Nonetheless I take my own advice and stay in the game, because I believe in love. But you all know it's hard out there. You look around, and you're in a dating pool filled with a bunch of crackheads and crazies—all the while hoping you're not one of them.

Then, if that weren't enough relationship stress—a business partnership and friendship I cherished came to an abrupt end. It broadsided me and left me feeling dejected and down. Professionally it put me at a crossroads, leaving me contemplating what to do next. Personally, it crushed me to my core, as it was completely unexpected.

Dealing with both personal and professional relationship disappointments at once was daunting. I am a firm believer in going to gratitude under any circumstance and keeping it moving. So that's what I did. I kept going and stayed grateful. Notwithstanding my commitment to doing so, I still had an emptiness that was left from my lackluster dating experiences and my ever-dissolving partnership.

If you don't believe in miracles, just look around you. About three weeks ago, I received an invitation from an Australian friend, who I met once two years ago, to come to Venice, Italy. Under most circumstances I would have been flattered by the invitation but politely declined. This, however, felt different. My spirit was screaming at me to accept the invitation to adventure.

I had no idea how much I needed this trip. Being in a city like Venice has caused me to confront some of the core issues and feelings I was dealing with regarding relationships. More importantly it has forced me to look within and pull out the things that I love about myself. It is, honestly, a city of pure magic. However, the awakening self-awareness and self-appreciation has been in major parts fueled by my conversations with my friend who knows very little about me. Having to speak in detail about myself—my goals, my dreams, my fears…my life—has been one of the most cathartic experiences of my lifetime.

As a result, I have been reminded of just who I am. And I'm remembering that I'm the pooh! In turn it has also caused me to seek and see inspiration in all that I encounter. Sitting at an outdoor café eating gelato breeds an inspirational moment. Listening to a virtuoso string ensemble play Vivaldi's *Four Seasons* is a garden for new creative expression. From the mundane to the exquisite, once I started lovin' on me again, I have come alive.

We get so consumed in everyone else's opinions and views of who we are that we forget there's only one human opinion that counts—our own. My pastor says, "If God is already impressed with you, who is left to impress?" I hear him, and once again, I'm living it. If God and I both love me, then that's all I really need. Everything else is just gravy. Now, I like gravy, but mashed potatoes without gravy are still great.

I know that my setting lends itself to these romantic musings and discoveries, but it doesn't matter if you're in Venice, Italy, or Venice, Florida. You can start loving on yourself again. Take a look at your awesomeness inside and out, and love on it!!! For it is the only way you will be whole enough to love anybody else.

In Toni Morrison's masterpiece novel, *Beloved*, the preacher, Baby Suggs, says it best in her sermon in the Clearing:

> In this here place, we flesh; flesh that weeps, laughs; flesh that dances on bare feet in grass. Love it. Love it hard….Love your hands! Love them! Raise them up and kiss them. Touch others with them, pat them together, stroke them on your face 'cause they don't love that either. You got to love it, you!

■ ■ ■

YOU MAKE YOU

Recently I've been on a slight edge, happy yet overwhelmed by a lot on my plate. One night I couldn't sleep because of all the things swimming in my head that needed to be done. Really, I was worried about how it was all going to get done and the outcome. Over the past couple of years, I have been focused on practicing living in the now, but like with everything, it takes practice. And then the other night, the solution hit me. You make you!

I believe in the divine placement of your life—everything happens for a reason. It just so happens that this week I had a meeting with a world-renowned, multi-bestselling spiritual healer. Like many of us, I believe in the power of self-healing in concept, but not quite in reality. I wanted to believe that I had the power. I say it over and over again, but I didn't actually believe it.

To be honest I didn't really want to go to the meeting. I had too much to do, and I had no faith in the outcome. However, I try to keep my word and mostly succeed. I went to the meeting with low expectations. The meeting discussion went fine, and then the spiritual healer talked to me and prayed for me. By the end of the meeting, I had a different opinion of him and of my own ability to make powerful change in my life.

For the first few hours after the meeting, I was in a bit of a daze. Not spaced out, but just lifted with great thoughts. Then I jumped back into my "life," which quickly made me lose the feeling of happiness and control that I had felt. Ultimately it led to a night where I couldn't sleep.

First, I began to contemplate all of the stuff I had to do. Then the worries that I had about work, finances, family, love, and so on crept into my thoughts. And it was keeping me up! I decided to try and meditate to see if I could settle my thoughts. I haven't been quite successful at meditation but have continued to try. After about an hour, my thoughts did settle, and instead of thinking about all of the things I had to do, I began to encourage myself. To list the things I'm grateful for and focus on what was good in my life. Then came the realization that my worry was misplaced, because none of the stuff I was worried about makes me who I am.

We worry so much about external things and circumstances that we forget these things have no relevance to who we really are. We've assigned false importance to things—tangible and intangible. In the process we forget that the core of who we are never changes as things do. The core of who you are is your spirit. It's the reason why the saying, "Everything always works out," is the truth.

When Deepak Chopra said, "You are a spiritual being having a human experience," I didn't quite get it. Now I do. All of those things that we place false value on are temporary. Success, fame, work, bills, debt, relationships all eventually change. But what doesn't change is that none of those things make you who you truly are. You make you!

■ ■ ■

FROM MY SISTER-FRIEND, LA RIVERS

Ooooooh, you want me to tell my age, LOL. I've known of Nathan since my sophomore year in college. He's gonna kill me for telling this story; however, here goes. I knew "of" Nathan, because in college I was a resident advisor, and one of my wonderful students who lived on the floor, who will remain nameless, came to my door late one finals evening lamenting over a man whom she'd been involved with. She was so in love with his essence and couldn't seem to study, as her mind was distracted by his manhood. I had to know who the man was whom this woman was levitating over, and the universe provided me with his presence a few years later when I met him, in person, in New York City. His college years were full of scholastic endeavors and a full social life, as was mine, and we had yet to cross paths. Finally, *I met this man! He was accomplished and eager to dive into the business of entertainment law. I'd since left the business, and on a whim and a referral, we met at Bar 89 in SoHo and have been inseparable ever since.*

Nathan and I have been all over the world together; however, the most fun story that I'm allowed to tell is one great night we met up in the Hamptons. He was there for business, and I was there for my birthday. Nathan and I traveled to a good friend's place for a summer birthday dinner, party, and after gathering. Let's just say I owe him my life, because with no navigation system, no lights, no direction, and no help, he managed to drive my drunk ass home to safety. I awoke safely, in bed, fully clothed with last night's dinner snacks beside me, with no judgments.

This *is why Nathan is the girl's best friend.* He *is* the *most emotionally honest man I've ever known. Nathan is the kind of friend who will guide you with a loving hand, without judgments and with solutions. He has so much faith in women and humanity, and he doesn't keep secrets about men from us. He gives it to us straight, no chaser, but with a bouquet of flowers and champagne post success. Nathan appreciates women and all of humanity.*

He is the ultimate humanist. I'd go as far as to call him an emotional activist. He wants you and everyone around him to feel good, and with his experience he knows what you need.

Nathan is honest and open. He is kind and consistent. He is a man who says what he means and means what he says. That is the kind of man every woman wants and every man wishes he could be. That in and of itself, to me, is profound. There is no value I could place on Nathan Hale. He is the ultimate. He complements me in my force of nature.

I've seen this man have an idea, gather a team, and execute it. I am so happy and blessed to have been a part of our first film together, Dirty Laundry. *A film that swept the American Black Film Festival and went on to be nominated for an NAACP Award. I hate to say this, but I've not met another man who does every single thing he says he's gonna do, and he includes his friends in every project. If you tell Nathan you're a painter, he will find you a structure to cover. He never lets you go, even when you let you go. He believes in the arrived you, beyond who you are in the now. How epic is that? Nathan is an action man. He never says no to your dream. He says yes, without resistance. He will find your solution, or he will create it. He always quotes Milton Berle. He says, "If opportunity doesn't knock, build a door." That is the ultimate coolest shit ever!!!*

About La Rivers—Spiritual gangster. Artist, lover, and friend. In exchanging my position as an entertainment executive for the stage I have discovered my love for wild plays, skilled writers, and a fiery pursuit of pleasure.

TREAT YOURSELF BETTER, SUPERWOMAN

It's a brand-new year and decade! I always find it funny how many people agonize over resolutions and all of the life overhauls they're going to do *this* year. I stopped making resolutions about two years ago when I realized that I got more discouraged when by midyear I'd forsaken all of them. Instead I resolve to try my best to always do better and be better.

One of my sister-friends, however, is a veteran resolution maker, and she asked me for some advice. I told her to make one resolution: "Treat yourself!" Of course, she laughed at me, recounting how often she treated herself to massages, manicures, the hairdresser, etc. She was right; my sister-friend had no problem pampering herself with all of the luxuries that women have come to love. But I was talking about something a little different. I wanted her to treat herself…better.

I think this statement offended her. Actually, I know she was offended. She was missing the point. I wasn't saying she was self-abusive or anything of the sort. Let me give you some background. My sister-friend is a divorced, single mother with a daughter and a long-time boyfriend she's been dating for four years. She is very successful and extremely driven in her career. And she still manages to volunteer at her daughter's school, is active in several charities, and supports her man in all that he does in his very busy career. She is superwoman with a capital *S*.

Throughout the year before she decided to make a resolution, there were countless times when we'd be talking or having lunch/dinner, and she was completely beat down. She was frazzled by all of the demands on her time, talents, and spirit. I'd give a pep talk, and she would somehow muster up more energy to go back in and tackle all that was before her. Soccer games, parent/teacher meetings, charity galas, business dinners—it was a parade of nonstop events with an occasional pedicure or trip to Louboutin in between as some sort of consolation prize.

It had an effect on all of her relationships. By the time she got home each day, her patience was short with her daughter, who was starting to struggle in school. She was becoming more and more frustrated with her boyfriend and his demands. And she was missing deadlines and important tasks in her career. And it was a direct result of her not treating herself better and putting herself first. My sister-friend needed to be in first position before her man, her career, and yes, her daughter too.

For mothers, I know it is a foreign concept to put anything before your children. But if you think about it, what good are you to your children if you're only giving them a fraction of who you are? You must first take care of yourself so that you approach each moment with your children, your partner, and everyone else in your life with the fullness of your being. It was clear she needed to treat herself better.

I suggested that she have two to three days every month that were solely hers. No daughter. No man. No career. And make them consecutive. Then you're getting that mani-pedi in peace and not racing to ballet class or to dinner. Then that massage means something, because you're not jumping back into the stress of your life—you'll have time to let it marinate and let its therapy take full effect on your body. When you return to your life, you're rejuvenated and ready to give all of you.

Of course, she thought that would be impossible. "Where would I find two days to myself?" When I broke down how easy it was to make it happen, she had to concede that I was right. She'd made it impossible in her mind, because once again she was putting everyone else's needs in front of her own. Her daughter would be fine—she could stay with a sitter, a relative, or with me (as I offered). Her man would certainly be fine—he was always away on business trips for weeks on end. And her career? She's the boss…enough said.

She agreed to try it for the first three months of the year! I predicted this would be something she implements throughout the year. I'll keep you posted on how it goes. In the meantime, I bet there some other women wearing the *S* on their chests, who need to resolve to treat themselves better this year! I hope you'll take my challenge too. In the meantime, *Happy New Year!!!!!*

(Update: My sister-friend did keep up with her self-care regimen and still does to this day. Her daughter is well-adjusted and sees her mother as an example of how putting yourself first is a requirement for you to function for everyone and everything else in your life. I'm proud of her.)

■ ■ ■

THE SANITY OF LOVE

Love is patient, love is kind. It does not envy, it does not boast, it is not proud. It does not dishonor others, it is not self-seeking, it is not easily angered, it keeps no record of wrongs. Love does not delight in evil but rejoices with the truth. It always protects, always trusts, always hopes, always perseveres. Love never fails.

— *1 Corinthians 13:4-7 (NIV)*

I believe that is the truest statement about love. In media and in real life, we are bombarded with so many images of disconcerted "love" that it's easy to forget the true essence of what it means to love and be loved. But if you just follow the simple words of that scripture, you're well on your way to a healthy and fulfilling relationship—romantic or otherwise.

Last week I overheard a conversation a young woman was having with her girlfriend at a restaurant. She was discussing her relationship with her boyfriend. She spoke of the constant fighting, the cheating, and the jockeying back and forth for the pole position in their relationship. "Girl, you know I gotta put his [butt] in check," she said in a celebratory tone. Then she said the thing that almost made me fall out of my chair: "But you know I like all the drama; it lets me know he loves me."

Basically, she implied that all the negative things going on in the relationship verified his love for her. It led me to think that so many of us get it twisted about the true nature of love. Love is sane, and what she was describing was not. However, instead of focusing on that insanity, my thoughts turned to the great examples of love in my life.

My first example of true love is my mother. I am very fortunate to have a mother who has that old-fashioned, "love you through anything" kind of love. It is the singular relationship in my life that I can say has consistently been an example of that 1 Corinthians scripture. And I don't take my mother's love for granted, as I have seen many parents who have not had the same unconditional and wide-open love my mother has shown me. I am so grateful to have that in my life; it has made all of the difference.

If you read this column regularly, you know I'm always bragging about my friends. I have pretty much had the same friends my entire life. While I love all of my friends equally, there are three friends who hold a near and dear place in my heart. I have known my best friends, Andrea,

Antonious, and Danielle, for forty-one-plus years, and they have never wavered in their friendship and love for me. It is almost unbelievable that I've never had a fight with any of them. Not even a major disagreement, and I even lived with Danielle.

I count those three friendships as a top blessing in my life. We're always supportive of one another no matter what. We tell one another the truth even if it's unpopular. Most importantly there's never been any jealousy or envy in any of those relationships. And that's pretty hard considering they are all rock stars with great talents. I couldn't have asked for purer relationships than with those three people. It really is all about love, always has been and always will be.

Recently I've experienced a disappointing ending to a friendship that I thought was solid. As I evaluated that failed relationship, I realized that if I had applied the standards of love set by my three best friends, I should've known the difference. Truly this relationship was the antithesis of that scripture on love. If we pay attention, we know the difference between a sane relationship and one that is not.

I have often said that, if you don't like my best friend Danielle, then there is something wrong with you. Quite frankly I have never met anyone who doesn't like her. She's gorgeous, smart, and a ball of fun. With that said, she'd experienced some difficult times in dating when we became adults. So much so that she believed she was never going to get married. I thought, "Well, if Dani can't find anyone, then it's a wrap for me."

Thankfully she met a great man! They've been married for over ten years, and throughout those years they have been an example of what it means to be truly committed to your partner and give him or her unconditional love. The way they look at each other still after three kids and years of marriage just makes me smile. She supports him, and he supports her. At his retirement party (from the NFL), the final statement of his speech summed it up for me: "The best decision I made in my life was marrying Danielle." And you knew he meant every word of it. My heart melted.

Real love is all around us! Even though we are constantly fed bad information about love, we all know what it is supposed to be and feel like. I refuse to believe that love is contentious, because I know it for myself. And no matter what anyone says or does, I will always believe in the sanity of love.

∎ ∎ ∎

WHAT ARE YOU DOING FOR YOU?

The season between Labor Day and Thanksgiving is a frantic one. The post summer, preholiday grind is one of the most grueling. It's also the time when the single summer heat begins to cool off and unattached people start looking for others to keep them warm. Too many of my friends get into fall/winter romances that usually thaw by spring, all the while forgetting about the relationship that matters the most—the relationship with self.

It is so easy to get consumed with our day-to-day living that we forget to take a moment to check in with ourselves. Our nature is to get it done, care for others, and press Repeat. If you're like me then, your to-do list is full by Monday morning, and you're off to the races the rest of the week. It's especially true if you live in a fast-paced urban city like New York or DC or Chicago. The rhythm can be relentless and, if you're not careful, will take a toll on not only your body but also your spirit.

For me this became abundantly true this past week when I found myself extremely ill for three days and stuck in a shuffle between my bed and my sofa. Being single made it worse, because there was no one to whine to or to get me some juice. Thankfully my friends came by when they could to drop things off and lend some support, but of course they couldn't stay long—they had to-do lists too.

As I sat feeling sorry for myself because I couldn't tackle the myriad of things I hadn't crossed out and because I was having to weather this storm alone, I got to thinking. It seemed like a pattern for me. I would work and push myself until my body forced me to sit down and pay attention. Thankfully God made my body a lot smarter than me. Although I was in pain, I ended up surrendering to the moment and accepting the forced rest.

Then, as I was flipping through the TV (bored), I came upon CNN and the most gruesome picture I have ever seen broadcast. The picture of Gaddafi's blown-out brains. I was mortified and disgusted! Immediately I turned the channel, but once an image like that enters your spirit, it is very difficult to move on or forget. I sat there upset that the programmers and producers of CNN didn't think better than not to have shown such a grizzly image.

It continued to disturb me throughout my illness. Then I spoke to a physician friend who explained to me what might be happening to my body. Turns out I had an issue where toxins/poisons had stored up in my body and needed to be released. She explained that was probably the cause of my feverishness, aches, and fatigue. She also explained that if it didn't exist on its own, I should see someone. Sparing you the details, they did in fact exit my body, and I immediately felt better.

Of course, being the type of person that I am, I couldn't just take it at face value. I had to interpret a deeper, more global meaning. It's been a pretty difficult year, and I've had to deal with clearing up some outstanding personal business, the end of business and personal relationships, and other not-so-pleasant things. All in all, I had to clean up my house and press Restart. Much needed, but it was heavy.

Then I began to think of the Gaddafi image and all of the images I choose to feed my spirit, particularly on the television. Add it all up, and it's a surprise that I'm not insane. I imagine that I'm more typical than atypical, which has brought me here. We can get so caught up in all of the running of the world and never stop to understand how much poison we are putting in our bodies and spirits. Some of it is unavoidable, while most of it is by choice.

We also get so caught up in maintaining our external relationships at home, work, and school and with our friends that we forget to check on the internal relationship we have with ourselves and with the universe that lives within us. This lack of focus causes all of those toxins and negative information to build up in our bodies and spirits with no forced release. It's allowed to fester and ultimately affects all of those relationships we work so hard to get and maintain. If you're not giving yourself your best you, then you certainly aren't giving it to anyone else.

This week and in the upcoming weeks, I want to challenge you (and myself) to ask the simple question, "What are you doing for you?" Ask it every day as a constant reminder that each day you need to take even the slightest moment and do something that is just for you! Something that uplifts your spirit, inspires you, makes you feel powerful or sexy…something that is selfishly, unapologetically all about you!

∎ ∎ ∎

FROM MY SISTER-FRIEND, DR. BRANDI KENNER-BELL

I have had this crazy, amazing, one-of-a-kind type of friend for over twenty-nine years. That's over half my life! We have known each other longer than we have not, and my life would not have been the same without him. Nathan and I met in seventh grade; looking back it was probably the beginning of the rest of our lives. We were starting a program for early enrollment into high-school level academics. But it was so much more than that. It was the best high school in the city, the smartest kids, the prettiest girls, the coolest guys, and we were ready! To say those years were formative is the understatement of the decade. There were many first, many lasts (thank goodness!), and so many laughs. We figured out so much about ourselves during that time and not without a lot of mistakes and missteps. What every girl needs during that time is a cheerleader. A person to pick her up when she falls ('cause you will fall, even if it's not in public) and remind her of how fabulous she is; a person to tell her the truth, especially when she doesn't want to hear it (but never in public!); a person who knows her secrets but would only use them to lift her up; and most importantly a person who would defend her to the death, especially against jealous heifers and catty bitches. This is why he is "The Girl's Best Friend!"

Nathan is the reason I know I'm fabulous. It's the best advice he has ever given me. During one of the most devastating, embarrassing moments of my young life that happened on a rigorous dance team of which we were both members Nathan stood up for me. Not only did he stand up for me in front of the coach and the entire team, but he also made sure I knew, publicly and privately, how fabulous I was. He erased any doubt I may have let enter my head. It was a lesson in resilience, and I will never forget it. The experience was humbling and empowering all at the same time. It was the first time this pretty, popular girl did not get what she wanted. It was Nathan's support and near rebellion that gave me the strength to endure it and hold my head up high to move past it. He is the best friend.

But I must say the best part about Nathan is the hilarity that surrounds him. There is never a lack of fun and foolishness when he is in the mix. Why else would I drive ten hours both ways in one weekend to attend a Halloween party that started in a tiny apartment where I wore silver bell bottoms; made and drank copious amounts of a mystery punch; then proceeded through the streets of Washington, DC, at two in the morning; and finally ended up on the floor in the hallway locked out of the previously mentioned tiny apartment? (Apparently, you should take your keys with you when you leave the house in drunken revelry. The building security was not as amused. But such has been my life with Nathan Hale Williams, a girl's very best friend.)

About Dr. Kenner-Bell—I'm a forty-something year-old doctor, who spent most of her life in school and training and can't wait to retire. Somewhere along the way, I got married to a boy and had two crazy boys of my own. I'm an armchair activist who loves to read, though the pile of unread books on my nightstand suggests otherwise.

SAVE YOURSELF FIRST

I recently tweeted, "Notice: Nathan is resigning from the People Pleasing business. Sorry if you missed out! It was an impossible career! And the benefits [were horrible]!" This was in response to being tired of consistently doing things for other people who weren't grateful and ultimately disregarding my own needs.

I think all too often we subvert our own needs for the needs of others. Particularly when it comes to relationships and family. We find ourselves trying to help our loved ones who don't want to be helped, motivate the unmotivated, and save those who don't want to be saved. All the while forgetting that the only person one can truly help, motivate, or save is oneself.

One of my sister-friends has been married for about six years. She has recently been having problems with her marriage. Her husband has consistently had issues holding a job, and although she was with him strong at first, it is clearly beginning to break her down. His issues have more to do with his fundamental shortcomings than with a struggling economy.

My sister-friend has two children and another on the way. I was talking to her about a month ago, and she was having a breakdown because she'd reached the edge. A very successful lawyer, she found herself not only bringing home the bacon, but also cooking it, and then cleaning up after. Her husband had completely checked out and she didn't know what to do.

It was clear that, as a result of his apathy, she'd begun to lose her way as well. She'd picked up weight. She no longer did the things that brought her joy. Each morning was a struggle for her to get out of bed, because the pressure and stress had completely debilitated her. Not to mention she had a new life growing inside her belly.

Feeling my sister-friend's pain, I gave her some advice that I almost always avoid giving. I told her that she should consider either moving out or asking him to leave. I am the biggest proponent of "till death do us part," but I am a bigger proponent of "you have to save yourself before you can help save anyone else." It was clear that her husband's energy was taking her over. The situation was not good for her, him, or their children.

Simply because he was uninspired, he no longer inspired my sister-friend to be her best self. And instead of her elevating him to be better, he was beginning to drag her down with him. She was missing lots of days at work and underperforming when she was there. Her saving grace is that she'd been a star, and she could blame the rough patch on the pregnancy. Nonetheless she wanted to make partner one day, and having any blemish on her record, baby or not, was not a good look.

My suggestion was that she separate herself from the toxicity of her husband's obvious depression and begin to surround herself with people who inspired and motivated her. In essence, she needed to get her "mojo" back, and it wasn't going to happen with her husband around.

I could sense her apprehension to my line of thinking and advice. She was a firm believer in "for better or worse." My response: "How much worse does it have to get for you to realize a change is necessary?" I wasn't advising her to divorce him. I was advising her to take a moment and save herself so she could help him and their family.

Had this been the first time this had happened, I would never have advised her to leave. However, this was yet another instance in a string of instances where he had failed the family. She'd hung in there time and time again, but now it was time to do something drastic. It had gotten to the point where either she made some hard decisions or they were going down together.

Ultimately, she took my advice and asked him to move out, and he did. For her it wasn't much of change because he'd checked out a long time ago. What has changed is that a major burden has been lifted off of her shoulders—his negative energy is now gone. She hadn't anticipated feeling as free and renewed as she does, but she's already getting some pep back in her step. All we are is energy, and when you're surrounded by negative energy, you can't help but to feel it and be affected by it.

We discussed that the goal here is for her to get back on track and fortify her spirit so that she can better deal with his issues, in the hope of saving their marriage. He's agreed to go to couple's and individual therapy, which they will start this month. In the meantime, she is regaining the fire that she'll need to weather the storm and fight for her family. Had she not gone about the business of saving herself first, who knows where they'd be now?

It is very difficult to be selfish when you see a loved one hurting or in pain, especially if it's your spouse or partner. We can try everything to save them from their dark clouds, but the minute someone's negativity starts affecting your spirit, the best thing you can do for that person and for you is to save yourself first.

■ ■ ■

LOVING YOU

"Loving you is easy 'cause you're beautiful…" are the opening lyrics to my favorite song by the late Minnie Ripperton. Her voice effortlessly soars across the melody like a bird. Many have tried to replicate, but few match the virtuosity that was Minnie. Yet it's not just about the vocals; the lyrics are also divine. In the song she's talking to a lover, but what about turning some of that same love around and loving you?

I've often said that self-love is the most important love you have in your life. Without it you can't fully love anyone else. I do think, however, that people don't really know how to love themselves completely. It's so much easier to love our partners, our family, and especially our children. We leave ourselves neglected in the process.

I was talking with one of my sister-friends in Los Angeles this week as we sat in her backyard in the hills of Bel Air. It was a sight to see, looking out over what I call "La La Land." She'd seen me do my morning ritual—stretch, drink water, ready the Daily Word, pray, and meditate. And she asked me whether I do that every day.

"Yes, the great majority of days I do the exact same thing, always when I'm at my home and mostly when I'm on the road," I explained. Last year I implemented this ritual in the thick of a tumultuous time. However, I recently added something to the ritual—telling myself the things that I love about me each morning. Just like gratitude, listing the things that I love about me helps me to focus on what is good and right in my life and being.

"I would feel weird doing that; it seems a bit narcissistic," she said. Why? We are quick to point out our flaws and the things that are wrong with us. We beat ourselves up so much about this failure or that misstep. But we don't celebrate our successes and spiritual triumphs nearly enough. And I wasn't talking mostly about physical characteristics either. (Although I do think I'm cute.) You know you better than anyone else. If you're not celebrating the good that lives in you, then no one will.

The practice helped me so much during a time when others were trying to paint me to be something I was not. If you know who you are, no one can convince you differently. Moreover, the world in general will try to define you based on your limitations, and the best way to overcome that is to trumpet your abilities. Each day I feel like I'm putting on my spiritual armor by first going to gratitude and then loving on me.

This morning she tried it, and she left the house feeling great and ready for the day. I can't wait to speak to her later to see if it made any difference in the rest of the day, but I do know she started with a pep in her step. And as with anything, practice makes perfect, which is why I practice it every day.

If you're feeling unloved, the first place to look is within. You are truly the only person you can control, and it's the purest love you can get. Try this practice out for the week, and get to the business of loving you!

(Update: This column was actually about a brother-friend. I am not sure if he still does this or for how long he continued to do this after that first day, however, he has left the job that made him unhappy for something that makes him excited. For me, reading this column again reminded me that I need to start doing this again myself. I had another business relationship that didn't quite work out as I planned and it caused me to doubt who I am. I had allowed the failure of the relationship to define me based on my limitations. Reading this column forced me to remember that I alone define who I am and it is certainly not based on the things I lack. It is based on the characteristics that are abundant in my spirit. Taking my own advice.)

■ ■ ■

DON'T LET ANYONE BRING YOU DOWN

Last week I had the privilege of seeing *A Streetcar Named Desire* on Broadway with a predominantly African-American cast. Nicole Ari Parker's (*Soul Food*) performance was astonishingly brilliant in the lead role of Blanche Dubois, a fading Southern beauty down on her "luck." Her command of the language, attitude, and pathos of the era transported the audience back to the time in which Tennessee Williams set the dramatic play. It struck me equally that many of the themes are contemporary themes that play out in today's society. One of the main themes that resonated with me was not to let anyone bring you down.

It was my first time seeing *Streetcar* in any form, and so I was surprised to discover that the entire play is about relationships. Blanche's sister, Stella (played by Daphne

Rubin-Vega), is married to a brute of a man, Stanley (Blair Underwood), who is a far cry from Blanche and Stella's high-society upbringing. As Blanche descends on Stella and Stanley, she is in full-on judgment of her sister's living conditions. Stanley is "common" and definitely not of the ilk intended for the Dubois sisters.

From the moment she arrives, Blanche begins to tear Stanley apart in private conversations with Stella, who had seemingly been content with her life before Blanche's arrival. I've seen this scene played out all too often in real life. I've repeatedly cautioned my sister-friends about letting outsiders into their relationships. As is the case with Blanche, the person throwing stones at your relationship lives in a fragile glass house and is reflecting his or her own personal drama on you and your relationship. And more often than not is jealous of what you have.

Unfortunately for Stella, her sister's quiet destruction of her relationship isn't her only problem. Despite her selfish motivations Blanche is right about Stanley. He is a drunken and abusive mess. It's not just his status in life that is beneath Stella, but also the way in which he treats her. Although I found Blair Underwood's portrayal too brutish with no sympathetic qualities, I could see how the character was written. Stanley has layers and is trying to do his best to survive his circumstances and too is not proud of his position in life. And when intoxicated, he takes this out on the person closest to him, Stella.

Both of these familiar plots made me think about how many of my sister-friends have let other people bring them down. Parker's virtuoso performance reveals how seemingly good intentions can have a bad foundation. She claims that her sole concern is her sister's well-being when in fact there are several ulterior motives at play. You have to be careful from whom you take relationship advice.

As I have said, the conflict in the play though is that most of what Blanche is saying is true. Stella has convinced herself that Stanley's excessive drinking and abuse is appropriate behavior. She has allowed their clear physical passion to override good judgment. Clearly his feelings of inferiority and failure lead him to attack Stella and her background. Instead of rising to a higher level, he is intent on bringing her down to his.

I found myself wanting to yell, "Stella!!!" throughout the entire play. I wanted to save her from two people hell-bent on destroying her life. Both of whom were in the dark depths of their lives and were in a tug-of-war to see who could drag her to their level first. It made me feel for all of my sister-friends in similar situations. I just encourage you not to be a Stella, and don't let anyone bring you down.

■ ■ ■

FROM MY SISTER-FRIEND, DANIELLE WALKER

Nathan knows essays are not my thing, but they are his (obviously). I'm more of a logic and logistics person—math, science, and engineering. But I couldn't resist the opportunity to tell you about my best friend of more than twenty-seven years, Nathan Hale Williams. We met as freshmen in high school, and Nathan would say, "Hey, pretty girl," every time I passed him in the hallway. Always the charmer, Nathan had that special something even in the awkward teenage years. Later that year we both auditioned for the Whitney M. Young High School's Dancing Guys-N-Dolls, our school's prestigious (and difficult) dance team. We both made it, and that sealed our friendship. We were definitely instant besties and have been ever since then.

For the past twenty-five-plus years, we have shared the highs and lows of life, so picking one funny story is certainly hard. If you know Nathan, then you know funny is always on the menu. But here's one story that is indicative of our wonderfully silly relationship. Nathan and I used to be roommates in our early twenties, and our apartment had a rather long hallway. When we got bored, we would dress up in mismatched clothes and accessorize in odd things from around the house (think spatula/ hairbrush/pillow stuffed in clothes). We'd walk that long hallway as if it were a high-fashion runway with serious faces and pouty mouths (we were smizing before Tyra ever taped the first episode of Top Model*), and we'd compete to see who was the fiercest and most outrageous. We would yell at each other (in an encouraging way), "You're not working the runway, honey!" It was ridiculous, and we loved every minute of it.*

The best piece of advice Nathan has ever given me was, "Remember your husband didn't marry a fat girl. Keep it tight and cute." At first glance that seems harsh, but if you know Nathan, it is par for the course. He keeps it real with you, and if you ever don't want to know the truth, do not ask Nathan. I love that about him though. All of his friends do. Nathan is not only insanely fun—the life of the party—he's also one of the most positive and encouraging people I have ever met. He is extremely loyal to those he loves, and he's not afraid to be honest or to show vulnerability, so you know you're getting the real deal.

About Danielle Walker—I am a wife and mother of three energetic boys, who think I am the queen of the universe. I received my MBA from the Wharton School at the University of Pennsylvania and a BS in electrical and computer engineering at the University of Illinois at Urbana-Champaign (where I was the top engineering student for five consecutive years). Currently, I run businesses with my husband and my home castle. [Note: NHW wrote Danielle's bio blurb—she is far too humble to write about how amazing she truly is.]

MY SISTER-FRIEND WHITNEY

Jokingly, I used to blame Whitney Houston for my often times idyllic thoughts about love. I learned about love from Whitney's music, and she was the first entertainer I loved. When I was younger, my mother made me go in the basement to sing "The Greatest Love of All," because *she* didn't love my voice. But when I was singing along with Whitney, I knew love was in the world.

Like many true Whitney fans, I was devastated and numbed by her sudden passing. Purposely I never met Whitney, because I didn't want to spoil the perfect image I had created of her. Yet since the late 1980s, Whitney and I connected every day through her music. She made me smile, happy, cry, and inspired, and she comforted me when I was down. In my mind she was my ultimate sister-friend.

Loving Whitney wasn't easy though, especially in the latter years of her life. I often found myself in the most heated discussions about her, defending her talent and legacy. For sure I wasn't a fair-weather friend, and if you know me, you know there are a few things you don't talk about: my mother, my family, my friends, and Whitney Houston. She was my girl. I didn't care to discuss the demons she was fighting—we all have demons. If you wanted to talk about Whitney with me, it had to be a celebration of what was exceptional about her. And there was plenty of that to talk about.

It's very touching to see that in her death, people are giving her what she is due. She was the greatest singer of our generation with unparalleled success. She broke down barriers for black people and women not only in entertainment, but also in society as a whole. Although she never boasted about her charitable work, her contributions to charitable causes were countless as well as her opposition to the ills of our world, like apartheid. She was a force (on and off the stage) the world had not seen and I believe we won't see again for quite some time.

With that said, Whitney's sudden death and the outpouring of posthumous support and praise is yet another reminder to give people roses while they're here to smell them. I wonder, if during life Whitney had felt the love she is getting since her death, would she have gone down the path that ultimately led to her untimely demise? As I mourn the loss of my sister-friend, I'm reminded to give and share love with those I love today, for tomorrow is not promised.

Whitney gave good love! She was all the woman I needed. But I know that her broken heart has found its way home. Thank you, Whitney Elizabeth Houston, for taking good care of my heart. For this I will always love you! Rest in peace, Nippy.

■ ■ ■

IT GETS BETTER

In 2010, the "It Gets Better" campaign started as a result of the onslaught of suicides by young LGBT teenagers and young adults. The mission of the campaign was to let these young folks know that despite the turmoil they were experiencing life does get better. Undoubtedly it was a message that helped save lives and it is one you might need to hear too.

Two years ago, one of my sister-friends found herself divorced with four children under ten years old. She had filed for bankruptcy and was living with her mother-in-law (of all people). In her eyes she had hit rock bottom—life had not worked out as she had planned. For my sister-friend it was a devastating place to be in; especially as a highly educated woman from an upper-middle class family.

Out of the blue her marriage had come to an abrupt end after discovering her husband had been cheating with his office clerk for almost five years of their seven-year marriage. It was too typical and completely cliché but true. After vehemently protesting the affair, she found herself with an empty bank account, locked out of her sprawling home. and the only thing left was a note from her "husband" saying she should expect divorce papers soon. To add insult to injury, a copy of her prenuptial agreement was attached to the note.

One day she called me at her wits end stating that she was contemplating suicide. We'd already spent many nights on the phone while she cried uncontrollably for hours. I let her weep and deal with the emotions because I believed that was the only way she was going to be able to release the pain. Over the months though, I hadn't seen a change and with this call I knew that enough was enough.

"That's not an option," I exclaimed! She was seeking more sympathy, which I didn't believe was going to be helpful. She was already wallowing in self-pity and it was becoming a conundrum from which she was not going to be able to recover. "Snap out of it, you're creating more pain for yourself by not pulling yourself together and moving forward. If you end your life, that's the end. No more living, no more anything. It's going to get better! It always does," I preached as hard as I could.

But I wasn't coming straight from a self-help book, even though I've read many. I was talking from my own experience. I too, a couple of years before, had found myself in a deep depression and didn't know how to get out of it. At the time, I didn't even realize I was depressed because as a black man that wasn't even a part of my vocabulary. The truth is I was very depressed and although I never fully contemplated suicide I understood it for the first time in my life.

During the time of my depression, the world was dark. For me it was stranger than normal because I'd lived most of my life in the light. Getting out of the bed was a chore, as well as, other simple things like showering. Thankfully I have a naturally resilient spirit and I fought as hard as I could to get to the other side.

"I've been where you are and I promise you that it may not seem like it, but there is a rainbow at the end of this storm," I shared. It was the truth! On the other side of my dark journey, I began to find the light again and in a brighter version than I ever had before. First, I had to deal with the issues that put me in the state of depression. In my case it was valuing myself based on material things and other people's valuation/praise. If you do that, and it goes away what are you left with when it does? Nothing.

For my sister-friend she had to get over the fact that life had not worked out as she had planned. Oh well! It rarely does for anyone. But that does not give you the right to give up on it. Moreover, with four kids anything except a fight to the end was selfish and weak. She had to accept her circumstances and turn those lemons into some sweet ass lemonade.

Thankfully with support from her family and friends she was able to find the strength inside of her that lives inside of all of us to survive. Two years later she has re-entered the workforce, fought for a substantial settlement from her husband, and is now engaged to a wonderful man who loves she and her children. (Much better guy than her ex-husband). When I see her now, I know the feeling she feels—true happiness. It's an awesome feeling especially following a storm.

During these rough times, both economic and societal, many of us are experiencing a strain on our spirits. Whether you are gay, lesbian or transgender in an unaccepting world or if you're a divorcee with the burden of raising a family alone please know that giving up is not an option. You must keep going because it *always* gets better!

■ ■ ■

TIME TO SCRAP YOUR FIVE-YEAR PLAN

We all know the line, "The best laid [plans] of mice and men often go awry." No truer statement could be said about making life plans both professional and personal. As a child, I was sure I would grow up to be a doctor. As an adult I was sure I would be a millionaire by the age of thirty-five. Neither came to pass, but because I've been flexible I've allowed my life to form in such a way that I could have never planned, and it's been great.

Young overachievers are often taught to make plans for their education and their careers. I began writing out my goals for my life when I was about thirteen years old and have never stopped. In fact, I have my goals for the first half of this year on the wall by my desk now. It is a great daily reminder and it keeps me focused, but I have learned not to be rigid in seeking to fulfill those goals. The main reason is because what is on that paper cannot take into account this thing we call life.

One of my sister-friends is equally driven and similarly has five-year and ten-year plans. She is an entrepreneur who started a floral business a little more than three years ago. She developed a business plan for the first five years, and then ten years. She also developed a plan for her personal life, which included getting married. When she created both plans they seemed reasonable and doable. She'd enjoyed success as a florist on the side while she worked in corporate America and she'd been in a long-term relationship that was headed toward marriage.

Then life happened. Mid-way through her first year of business one of her main investors dropped out leaving her cash strapped. She struggled to find new capital to run the business and never fully recouped the intended capital she'd lost. She kept going and the business was decent. Her floral shop is located in lower Manhattan and when hurricane Irene came she was affected, but not devastatingly so. Hurricane Sandy was a completely different story—and it put her out of business for over a month.

Moreover, the strain on her business started to take a toll on her relationship, which ended in January. I certainly don't believe in giving up, but it was clear that an adjustment needed to be made. Instead of looking at her five-year plan as a failure it was time that she made a new one. The circumstances that were beyond her control prevented her from achieving the plan she had set so it was definitely time to make a new one based on the cards she'd been dealt.

It's easier said than done when you've encountered difficulties that leave you feeling defeated. But, the best thing about life is that you always can start over, make new plans, and keep going. I encouraged her to do just that and she has begun to do so. She is closing down her business by liquidating the assets and she has decided to do private floral services for catering companies and event planners, which she can do from her home or a small, lower-rent office. And I told her that she should start dating again.

There comes a point when you have to take an honest look at your plans and determine whether it's working or not. If you're like my sister-friend and it's not, then it might be time for you scrap that plan and start over. By all means whatever you do…keep going.

(Update: My sister-friend's business is thriving. She has opened up two locations in our hometown of Chicago. She is still single, but actively dating. I know that in due time that part of her life will work out too.)

■ ■ ■

CLOSE THAT OLD CHAPTER

This week marks the beginning of the Chinese New Year. I'm particularly excited because it is the year of the "Black Water Dragon." And according to Chinese astrology, I am a dragon. With every new year, Chinese or otherwise, we all look to leave things in the past in order to move on to new and better situations. This should be true in our love lives too—out with the old and in with the new!

I went shopping with my sister-friend this past week and we were talking about the new man in her life. He's European and they've been dating for six months. Although she's known him for over two years their relationship was completely unexpected to her. She never thought he could be her man. Yet there she was, all aglow and giddy like a schoolgirl.

It was great to see my sister-friend in such high spirits over love because I hadn't seen her like this since she'd met her ex-boyfriend over ten years ago. Sure, there were guys that she dated for various durations—two months here, six months there, but never anything that came close to the emotions she showed and shared about her ex. In fact, it had always been in the back of her mind that they'd one day get back together.

In fact, last November after a year of getting her personal house in order my sister-friend decided that it was time to explore dating her ex again. For all intents and purposes, they had a wonderful eight-year relationship and got along very well. She'd broken up with him (or at least she thought) purely because she needed space to find her personal identity.

She asked him out to lunch and they chatted about the world, their relationship, and the possibility of getting back together. It wasn't the first time they'd done this, but it was the most frank and direct conversation they'd had about it. Ultimately, they began to argue, which was rare for them. Leaving my sister-friend with the realization that it was much more than her needing to find her personal identity that had prompted her to leave.

"It was weird, in an instant I looked at him and thought, 'You're not my man,'" she said as we strolled through the racks at Saks Fifth Avenue. She went on to describe that because she had clarity in other aspects of her life she was able to see him, their relationship, and herself clearly. By the end of the conversation, she no longer had any intimate feelings for him beyond wanting to be great friends.

"You were romanticizing what you all had, so in your mind you'd forgotten all of the things that separated you and focused on the good," I added to the mix. And it was true. Every time she spoke of their relationship she had selective memory, which had kept the chapter open. But, I remember how upsetting his lack of passion was to her and how they just spoke a different love language from the beginning. Two great people just not made for each other.

The miraculous thing that happened was that once she closed that chapter she had even greater clarity. She was dating a couple of other guys and ended all of those relationships because now she was focused on what she wanted. More importantly she was open to seeing that what she wanted had been right in front of her for months—her current boyfriend.

Holding on to the past is generally a bad thing, especially in relationships. If you're still stuck in the past there is no way you can appreciate and enjoy the present. If you find yourself hung up on an ex it might be time for you to close that old chapter and start a new one.

(Update: More of a confession than an update. This one was about me. I'll leave it there to protect the innocent.)

■ ■ ■

FROM MY SISTER-FRIEND, RAQUEL "ROCKY" MALDONALDO

I met Nathan at Whitney M. Young High School in Chicago, Illinois in 1990. We met in the dance room of the school, as we were both auditioning for the school's dance team, 'Dancing Guys-N-Dolls.' Then, we both attended the University of Illinois at Urbana-Champaign.

One of the many funny Nathan stories occurred while we were in college. During our collegiate years, we would have to walk back to the dorms at the end of a great night of dancing. We would all act like supermodels (Nathan likes to do this a lot) and walk down the middle of the street like it was a runway. As we each took our turn to do the runway walk, like all of the great divas, the rest of us would sing RuPaul's hit song, "Supermodel." Screaming at each other, "You better WORK, cover girl, work it girl, give us a twirl, do your thang on the run way, Work, supermodel, work it girl." It was so much fun, as are most times hanging out with Nathan, who is unapologetic about who he is.

The best piece of advice he gave me came recently. He reminded me to take time to focus on the joy and disregard the negative people. Nathan is the Girl's Best friend because he greatly admires women because of his love for his mother. He loves to surround himself with divas of all kinds. His unconditional support and love for me has stood the test of time and distance. He wants the best for me and the rest of circle of friends.

About Raquel Maldonado—I am a Puerto Rican mother of two wonderful boys. I am a Chicago Park District Park Supervisor, where I spread my love of dance and fitness to youth and adults. I have a Bachelor of Science in Leisure Studies/ Recreation Management and a Master's in Education.

BE THE ONE THAT GOT AWAY

We've all had it happen. The moment when you run into an ex when they're looking good, seem happy, and make you feel tingly inside. Right then, you question yourself, "I let that go because of what?" Conversely, we all want ex-partners to feel the same way about us especially if you're the one that got dumped.

Last year my sister-friend got dumped via e-mail. It was a short message that the guy she'd been dating for eleven months no longer wanted to be with her. He was shipping her things to her apartment and basically said he no longer wanted to communicate with her in any capacity. As you can imagine, this was a major blow to my sister-friend's ego and she was extremely hurt by it.

Some other sister-friends and I came to the rescue with our best cheer her up. The dumping came out of left field and the manner in which he did it was so harsh. My other sister-friends wanted revenge and started plotting the guy's demise. Tires slashed. Showing out at his job. Nasty text messages. Hell, certainly has no fury like a woman scorned, especially when she's got some vindictive friends.

"Y'all are trying to go *Two Can Play That Game* on him, damn," I said jokingly. I offered this: "Someone once told me that the best revenge is good living." I then added, "The best revenge for an ex is good looking." I encouraged her not to give him or the situation more energy than either deserved. Instead, she should take this opportunity to turn lemons into lemonade. (For the record I wrote this column way before Beyoncé made *Lemonade*.)

She should put the energy into herself. During their relationship she did what many of us do and wasn't working out as much. She traded in the evening work out sessions for romantic dinners and drinks. And after a few months, she wasn't as tight as she was at the beginning of the relationship. Moreover, her world had been consumed by dating him and she'd let some of her on-the-side business projects go. I knew it would serve her spirit a world of good to reengage in her own life and not wallow.

My sister-friend decided to take my advice (and not slash his tires) and shook it off. She got back to her regular workout regimen. Jumped back into developing her business and almost immediately started dating again. Dating is like riding a horse. If you fall off, the best thing to do is to brush yourself off, get back up, and ride again.

Fast forward to last week and we were in the Meatpacking District of New York City with her new boyfriend and other friends having drinks outside. And lo and behold, guess who we see walking down the street? E-mail jerk. As he approached I could see my sister-friend's shoulders pull up.

When he got to our table it was written all over his face. He'd messed up. My sister-friend looked great, felt great, and had a hunk on her side. He, on the other hand, looked like he'd just walked through a car wash and had added a few pounds. I could feel the triumph she felt as he tripped over his words, looked her up and down, and then, high-tailed it out of there.

We've all been dumped before—all of us. It's not a great feeling and in the moment, you want revenge. However, instead of doing anything heinous the best thing to do is be the one that got away.

■ ■ ■

IS YOUR ENERGY OPEN?

A few years ago, I was experiencing some prolonged depression. At the time I didn't realize I was depressed as depression was not a part of my vocabulary. While I was feeling down I started searching for some answers—something to make me feel better. I had not long been a student of the self-help school, but I found some very helpful concepts in the books I read.

Two of those books were *The Secret* and *A New Earth*. Both books discussed the power and importance of energy. The energy you put out into the universe is what you get back. Like I said I was not a "nam myoho renge kyo" type of guy, but there was something to this whole energy thing. Since I first read both books, I firmly believe your energy and your thoughts are everything.

I have this sister-friend who has great, happy energy. She is a joy to be around and is always bringing positive vibes to situations. She is the type of person that makes you smile when you think of her. She's just that nice and caring. My other friends and I have been trying to set her up for the longest time, but with no luck.

Another friend and I were talking about my sister-friend because we were perplexed by her inability to score a date. Not dates, but *a* date. All of the ingredients are there. She is attractive, smart, and has an outstanding personality. So, what was the problem? As we talked more, it became clearer to me what was going on with my girl.

I had not realized that my sister-friend had some deep-rooted body image issues. I understand why my girls don't talk about these things with me, but my other friend articulated that my sister-friend has never felt comfortable with her body. I would never have guessed that because she always seems so confident about everything.

My sister-friend may not have a model's body, but most people don't. She has curves! Most women I know have curves and they don't have a hard time scoring dates. Men like curves, especially men of color. It wasn't what men thought of her curves, which was the problem. The problem was what she thought of them that was getting in her way.

Despite my sister-friends great, happy energy with us she does give off a different energy when it comes to men. In the back of her mind she had closed herself off to men and it came through when she met them. She had built up a wall based in fear, which emitted the "don't come over here" energy that kept men away. She'd defeated herself before she got in the game.

Being the meddlesome friend I am, I called my sister-friend to talk. My first question was, "Is your energy open when it comes to dating?"

She said, "Yes, I would really like to find someone."

But, "Is your energy open? When you're approached what are you saying to yourself?" She began to think about the question.

Turns out she was feeding her spirit bad information causing her to be closed off from guys. She recounted how when she'd been approached recently by a guy all of the negative things that would enter her mind. She went through a litany of reasons why whichever guy that had approached at the time was not going to like her. "He just wants to be friends." "He's trying to make nice with me to get with my girl." "Wait till he sees me without these Spanks on."

We can feel each other's energy even if we are unaware of it. She wasn't having any luck because she wasn't open. I asked, "Have you ever seen a busted chick with a fine guy and wondered, how did she get him?" She had great, confident energy that's how she got him. She believed she could. And it was fine time that my sister-friend started believing she could too.

I asked her to go through the exercise of changing the information she fed to her spirit the next time she was out and met a guy. We don't live in the same city, but the reports are that she is much more comfortable around guys.

So, I am hoping she scores her first date (in two years) very soon. Yes, I said two years!

If you're having a problem connecting when you meet guys maybe you need to check what energy you're putting out. It's possible that you're feeding your spirit negative thoughts, which block your ability to connect. Those bad thoughts send a message to your spirit to close off. Next time when you're meeting a guy you're interested in ask yourself, "Is [my] energy open?" And if it's not…open it!

(Update: My sister-friend is happily married. She opened her energy and met the man of her dreams. I am so happy for them.)

■ ■ ■

DON'T LOSE YOUR SWAGGER SISTER-FRIEND

I love black women! I said it in my very first *The Girl's Best Friend* column. I love everything about black women, especially those distinctive little things that make black women "sistahs." Don't get me wrong; I love everyone—all women. But, I have a special something for my sistahs, which is why I'm tired of people telling you not to be yourself.

One of my sister-friends and I were out for a night on the town. We met for drinks at one of our favorite bars in New York. My sister-friend is what you would've called a fly girl back in the 80s & 90s. Everything about her is on point. She's a successful attorney (we met when we were both in law school). She's also one of the most hilarious people you'll ever meet. It doesn't hurt that she's extremely easy on the eyes and always dipped in the "flyest" gear.

For the most part, my sister-friend doesn't have a hard time finding guys to date—they flock like pigeons. The problem is that she can't seem to find a man that meets her standards *and* accepts the colors of her personality. On the one hand, she can't date just any man because of her socio-economic status. On the other hand, the guys in her tax bracket or above can't cope with her raw and real personality. She's tried to date white guys who love that she "keeps it real," but that hasn't worked in step with her vision for her life.

Currently single, sister-friend and I began to discuss all of these books as well as the studies that continue to try to paint black women as broken and undesirable. She actually hates when men give women advice on relationships and "how-to-be." Naturally, this column is an exception. "Seriously Nathan, you are one of the few because you come from a place of love and not bashing us. I'm quite sick of the hate on us," she said. Well, I am too.

She told me the story of one black guy she dated who is affluent and successful. They'd gone out to a comedy show in a mainstream comedy club in New York City. If you've ever been to a comedy show with a black person you know we love to get it in and have a great time. My sister-friend said she was enjoying herself, laughing loudly; and, figuratively falling out of her chair—as we do. Her date was mortified and did not hesitate to tell her so.

"Did you have to be so ghetto? Just so you know, I'm not looking for one of those head rolling, finger snapping black chicks. I went to Yale," he said attempting to educate her. Wrong move, Bruh. Wrong move. First, there is nothing about my sister-friend that is "ghetto." Like I said, she does keep it real and she is very authentic to who she is. She has that natural sistah-girl swagger, but by no means is she ever crass or inappropriate. With that said, I'm surprised she didn't clock homeboy. She did let him know though.

Once again, another man discrediting black women based on generalizations and stereotypes. I told her, "He's a jerk and will probably not end up with a black woman anyway. 'Cause if you love black women it is their swagger that distinguishes them and you love it." I encouraged her not to change a thing about who she is because it was born from centuries of strength, resilience, and confidence. It was necessary to survive the oppression of the world and still raise families, work, and live.

To be clear I'm not talking about a bad attitude. Bad attitudes are toxic and black women don't monopolize the market for bad attitudes. Bad attitudes come in white, black, Asian, Latina and so on. I think the commentators confuse bad attitude with something that is pure and in the cultural DNA of most black women. It's that intangible thing that we all know black women own.

The late Dr. Maya Angelou states it the best in her poem, "Phenomenal Woman:"

> It's the fire in my eyes,
> And, the flash of my teeth,
> The swing in my waist,
> And, the joy in my feet.

Oprah Winfrey packaged it and sold it to millions of women (mostly white) every day for twenty-five years. It made her a billionaire and one of the most influential women in the world. Because Oprah wasn't afraid to let it flow and let her "sistah swagger" show she was able to present and discuss topics that had been previously been taboo on daytime talk television. She embraced it and celebrated it by just being herself.

Like my sister-friend, I am tired of people trying to strip black women of that thing that distinguishes you and makes you special. There is nothing wrong with you. You are strength. You are inspiration. You are love. You rock—just the way you are. The next time some comedian or research study tells you you're broken and no one wants you, just remember that your essence is wonderful and by all means please don't lose your swagger sister-friend.

■ ■ ■

SINGLE LADIES—DATING

"'Cause if you liked it, you should've put a ring on it."

—Beyoncé

"We come to love not by finding a perfect person, but by learning to see an imperfect person perfectly."

—Sam Keen

KNOW YOUR STANDARDS

I despise the grocery store, but one of the lessons I wish I had learned from my mother is how to grocery shop. My mother is meticulous about everything. With grocery shopping though, she takes it to the next level. Whether it be produce, meats. or bread she painstakingly selects the best quality for the best price. She has standards and anything she buys must meet those standards.

About twelve years ago, my best friend Danielle said to me that she only wanted to marry a man whose parents were still married. At first this offended me because my parents are divorced and I consider myself pretty grounded. Most days.

Over the years I have come to understand why she said that and what she meant. She wanted to marry a man who had a model of a successful marriage from which he could reference in their prospective relationship. It was a standard she had set for herself and her future husband. Thankfully, she found a man that met her standards and they've been happily married for over a decade.

One of my other sister-friends has not been so lucky in love. Her eight-year marriage ended in divorce. She's been dating a guy for about four months, but they're constantly having problems. He's not a bad guy, but they've been arguing from day one. It's out of character for my sister-friend to be contentious with anyone let alone someone she's dating.

Perplexed by the relationship, my sister-friend asked what she should do about this guy. On the one hand, she really enjoyed their time together…when they weren't arguing. On the other hand, she knew they argued much too often. I asked her, "Do you know your standards?" She quickly replied, "Yes, of course." The question is not as simple as she thought and I challenged her to think about it a little deeper.

"I don't mean height, hair color, and so on. Do you know what your standards are beyond the superficial?" What type of family background does your ideal man have? Education? Cultural interests? Relationship with his family? Spirituality? Exercise and fitness goals? Political views? And the list goes on depending on what was important to her.

My sister-friend who is pretty easy going thought I was being "too rigid." She'd been reading those so-called advice books for women that told her to be more flexible in what she was willing to accept from a man. I couldn't disagree more. Why should *she* be flexible in her standards? Most men certainly are not.

To put it plainly, I went to my not so-inner alpha male. I said, "If you were going to buy a car do you just show up at any car dealer and hope for the best? No! You set some standards or criteria for the type of car you're looking for." If you're a Mercedes kind of person, you're wasting your time at Hyundai. Once you've set your standards, it is easier to determine which car is right or wrong for you. Not to say you don't have flexibility—so instead of a Mercedes you might get a Beamer, but you certainly don't buy a Yugo.

The same is true in dating. How could my sister-friend avoid getting guys that didn't meet her standards if she didn't know them for herself? Quite frankly, the reason why she and the guy were arguing all of the time was because he did not fundamentally meet her standards.

My sister-friend is an eternal optimist. The guy she is dating is consistently pessimistic. She is highly educated. He's educated, but not at the intellectual level of my friend. Her idea of a good night was a movie and dinner. He liked to party all the time. She's ambitious. He's content. She goes to church every Sunday. He hadn't been to church in years. You see where I am going with this—she had no business dating him in the first place.

I would never tell one of my sister-friends not to date a guy. People need to reach those conclusions on their own. What I did instead was to point out the many deficiencies in their relationship and it all stemmed from her not properly defining and knowing her own standards. The guy was handsome, fun and "not psycho." All too often I see my girls settling for "not psycho" in lieu of what they really want.

I don't know if she will end it with the guy or not, but she has made a list of her standards. She has said it has made the world of difference in her thinking about dating. It has also put an even further strain on their relationship as she is more aware that the guy just doesn't cut it. Whatever she decides about the relationship going forward she now has a barometer by which she can evaluate him and the next guy she meets.

In order to get what you want you have to know what you want. I firmly believe that setting your standards for your ideal man is a manifestation that he will come and you will get him. Settling for someone who does not meet those standards does no good. But, you first have to know your standards before anyone can meet them.

■ ■ ■

GOOD MEN STILL EXIST

"All the good men are either taken, gay, or don't like black women," is a statement that I have heard far too many times. The fact is that it's just not true. Not only do I know plenty of heterosexual, single men who like black women, but I'm constantly meeting even more that I did not know. I really believe in the power of intention as well as the laws of attraction and I think some of that statement becomes a self-fulfilling prophesy.

Recently, at a party at my friend's house two of my sister-friends were discussing the status of men in New York, particularly black men. One of my sister-friends vehemently criticized the men that she'd encountered for not being up to par. In her eyes there was an abundance of jerks out there and a scarcity of the proverbial "good man." It was clear that she was embittered by her experiences while dating in the big apple.

My other sister-friend could not have disagreed with her more. Her reality was a stark contrast to the bitter sister. She said she had no problems finding men of quality and challenged my other friend to think about her perspective. She reminded her that she was in a house full of the type of guys she was looking for—successful, attractive, kind, and interested in a commitment. Even if they weren't directly interested in her she highlighted the fact that birds of a feather flock together.

As the discussion ramped up two of the single guys there jumped into the conversation. They agreed with my positive minded sister-friend that maybe the other's approach was preventing her from meeting the type of guys she wanted. Although I stayed out of the discussion and enjoyed watching, I too believe that the energy that my sister-friend was putting out was the primary reason why she was not attracting the right guy. By going into any situation with such a negative attitude about men in general was definitely not the honey that gets a good bee's attention.

I get tired of the black man bashing that happens too frequently. Sure, there are some rotten apples out there, but that doesn't make the entire bushel rotten. Being a black man in America in of itself is a struggle for a myriad of reasons. If our own sisters believe that there aren't any of us left that are good, then how do we expect the rest of our society to respect us? It's upsetting because exemplary men who are the quintessential man surround me and many of them are single. I know firsthand that my sister-friend is incorrect.

I hope the discussion encouraged my sister-friend to reassess her evaluation of men. By limiting her opinion to the men she'd dated she mistakenly lumped all men together. With this approach I strongly believe that she was blocking herself from meeting the type of guy of which she dreamed. No "good man" wants a woman that doesn't believe he exists.

■ ■ ■

LOVE AT FIRST SIGHT

Love songs really messed me up. I grew up listening to Whitney, Anita, Luther, Mariah and even Celine Dion (just in case you needed her last name). It was a time when the love in music talked about fairy tale beginnings and endings. True, there were some sad songs, but the hope that was found in the music of the aforementioned recording artists contributed to making me a hopeless romantic. For this reason, I have always believed in (and have experienced) the idyllic concept of love at first sight.

I was on the phone with one of my closest sister-friends who had been single for a little over three years. From the moment we got on the phone I could hear the excitement in her voice. After we finished the initial small talk about work and life I had to ask, "What has you so happy?" She giggled through the telephone, which was odd because this sister-friend is not the giggly type.

"I met a guy and I think he's the one," she said reluctantly. I asked when they'd met and again, with some hesitation she replied, "two weeks ago. I know it sounds silly, but there's something about him that is just right. We instantly clicked and have been inseparable ever since. I think I'm in love."

As much as I wasn't expecting that I could hear that she was serious. And like I said, this was one of my more serious sister-friends who always means what she says. "Well, I don't think it's silly, it's quite possible. It's happened to me before and I ended up in an eight-year relationship."

"I know, but it's a bit confusing," she said. She was very concerned that it was just the excitement of meeting someone who had all of her boxes checked in her "Love to Do List" (she reads my column faithfully). But, then again as she spoke more about it, the connection seemed far more spiritual and esoteric than a laundry list of attributes. According to her it felt as if she'd known him for many years, and it felt as if he'd been waiting for her all of his life. And she for him.

The hopeless romantic kicked in and my heart couldn't help, but to warm. Rihanna's current hit, "Where Have You Been" is far less romantic, but hits the nail on the head. My sister-friend had met the guy she'd been looking for her entire life. Isn't that what we all dream of and hope for in love. Yes, we can confuse some other feelings like lust for love, but with my sister-friend I don't think this is the case. She is a very cautious person and is extremely self-aware.

To ease her concern and fear, I ran down all of my friends who had experienced the wonderful phenomenon of love at first sight. Coincidentally, most of the friends I know that this has happened to are still in loving, successful relationships with their partners. The ones that aren't had long lasting relationships that ended and developed into fantastic friendships like my relationship that started with love at first. The best advice I could give her was to live in the moment and enjoy herself. Truly, it is all we can do in any situation, love or life.

We've all become so cynical and cautious about something as complexly wonderful as love. Some of it's justified, but I like to believe in those songs that I grew up listening to as a younger person. I was happy I could encourage my friend having experienced and seen it for myself, which is why I completely believe in love at first sight.

(Update: I hate to be the bearer of bad news, but this relationship didn't work out for my sister-friend. It did for a long while even leading to an engagement. The problem was that the more she knew about her fiancé the less she liked. She had the good sense to get off of the train before it went to the point of marriage. The good news is she has been dating another guy for three years now. I do think the previous relationship has made her gun shy this time around, but I am hopeful that she will soon be able to fully believe in the power of love again.)

■ ■ ■

DUTCH IS FOR AMSTERDAM

Last night one of my sister-friends took all of our friends out to dinner. She was the only female at the table of five. Normally, I would feel very uncomfortable about this—a table full of guys and the woman pays. I do understand that part of my discomfort is rooted in some antiquated and borderline chauvinistic ideals. I prefer to look at them as me being a gentleman. It's something I debate constantly in these situations. Thankfully, she owns the restaurant so it was ultimately not a big deal. With that said I don't mind being called old fashioned when it comes to dating. I don't understand the whole concept of going "Dutch," on dates especially first dates.

Another one of my sister-friends called me this week flabbergasted. She'd gone out with a guy for dinner and he suggested that they "split the bill." Granted, my sister-friend does very well for herself, but the guy she went out with has a good job too. More importantly, he asked *her* out on the date. I totally understood why she was upset, but her date didn't get it.

I know we're in new age times when it comes to dating and sisters are doing it for themselves. However, there are just certain things that shouldn't change. In any man's company, my mother will wait at a door until it is opened for her. She quietly demands it and I respect her for it. I say to my sister-friends, "Don't touch that door I got it." I was taught to be a gentleman and I don't think that diminishes a woman's independence.

My sister-friend's date argued that since women were "liberated" in so many respects these days it was completely acceptable for him to ask her to split the check. "That's some bull [crap]," I said.

As she told me, this is the same guy that said, "I'm looking for a woman who could cook as good as my momma." And, he couldn't pay for dinner. It was a hypocritical double standard to say the least.

I sincerely believe that you get the respect you demand. I applauded my sister-friend for refusing to go "Dutch" and insisting that he pay for the meal. After which, she not so politely told him to lose her number. Good for her! Yet, it got me to thinking, 'How many women hadn't been so resolute and pulled out their wallets to pay?' I imagine that had happened before and there'd been some women that had continued to date this jerk.

Yes, women have come a long way from bare foot, pregnant, and in the kitchen. I think there should still be a level of chivalry in dating between a man and a woman. If a guy is not on his very best behavior from the outset, then it's only going downhill from there. He should be bending over backwards trying to impress you—including wining and dining you. In my book, that is the bare minimum. And no, dinner is not an entitlement to sex, even if you did order the surf and turf.

Men will try to get away with whatever they can. I'm a man and I admit this truth. I do think too many women have let men get away with way too much. All the news reports and 'studies' have you lowering your expectations and standards. Stop it! Right now! You deserve better! You deserve to be treated like a lady regardless of your title at work. The next time some guy suggests you 'split it,' tell him "Dutch is for Amsterdam," and scram!

■ ■ ■

AIN'T NOTHIN' GOIN' ON BUT THE RENT

"No romance, without finance. 'Cause ain't nothin' going on, but the rent!" If you're thirty-five plus, you definitely remember the late Gwen Guthrie's 1986 anthem. You couldn't go anywhere without hearing that song on the radio.

My memory of the song was from my mother's friend and co-worker, Cre. She was a self-defined "fly-girl" and it was clear you had to have a "j-o-b," if you wanted to be with her. Actually, that was a non-negotiable requirement for all of the women who were single while I was growing up. If you were dating a man he better at least be *able* to help with some bills.

Fast-forward to 2011 and we all know that sisters outpace black men in educational and economic growth. The rent's still going on, but women aren't as reliant on men to make it happen. Sisters are doing it for themselves. Gwen's song is a bit out of place these days. Or, is it?

One of my sister-friends has been dating a very successful plastic surgeon for over three years. She works in publishing and has two kids from her previous marriage. Her ex-husband is also a rich man and supports the kids, but she does not receive alimony. Child support and the men her life aside she has achieved success in her own right and holds her own.

The recession hit everyone and every industry. Publishing was one of the hardest hit because not only did it have to deal with the general recession, but the industry also faced competition from the Internet decreasing the sales of books and magazines. My sister-friend was not immune to this hit and found herself dipping more and more into her investments after she'd been laid off from her six-figure income job.

One day my sister-friend called me and as we were talking she started snapping at me. Completely out of the blue and not based on anything I had done. I asked her what was wrong and after some coaxing she relayed that she'd lost a bunch of money in the market over the past month. And she wasn't sure she could afford her apartment anymore.

First, I gave my go-to pep talk of, "God's got your back. He won't give you more than you can bear! Stay optimistic…yadda, yadda." Then I asked her, "Have you lost your mind?" She was confused. "Isn't your man worth around fifteen million dollars…on a bad day?" She replied, "Yes, but I can't ask him for help."

She was very concerned that the perception would be that she was after his money. It had been an issue for him in the past and coming off of a divorce from another highly successful guy she did not want him to think that was her motivation. My response, "Sweetheart, brothas in the 'hood pay bills. So, should yours!"

Somewhere along the independent woman journey she lost her good sense. Every other aspect of their relationship was "traditional." She did the cooking when they shared the same space. She organized his clothes, did laundry, made appointments for him, and so on. Basically, she fulfilled the traditional role of wife without the title. But, she wasn't getting the traditional benefits of being a wife—not having to go it alone—especially when it came to finances.

I did not understand it. He was sitting on a pile of cash and could easily help her out. And he should be happy to do so. The problem was that he didn't even have a clue she was experiencing any difficulties because she had not told him. He assumed she had it under control.

I do understand, however, the difficulty in modern times for women to balance independence and their expectations of men. I think the great majority of women want "traditional" relationships in that they want families and they want to care for them. I still think it has gotten twisted.

The men in your life should be supporting you in all aspects of your life and not just financially. He should be helping with childcare if there are children involved (whether they are his kids or not). He should be helping you live your best life and you should not be suffering alone. What's the point in being in a relationship if you don't support each other?

I told my sister-friend to get over herself and ask him for help. Of course, he was more than willing to lend a bridge to her while she regrouped. He then set up a regular system each month to help her pay down her debt and her bills. Exactly! Once she stopped playing by some made-up rich people rules and got her good sense back she was less stressed. And they're getting married next year.

If you have a man in your life that is not helping you out—no matter what your situation is, then you need to reevaluate your relationship. I think he should be offering to help you and not put the burden on you to ask. If he's not maybe you should dust off your cassette tape and play him Gwen Guthrie's hit, "'Cause ain't nothing going on, but the rent."

■ ■ ■

HE GOOGLED ME

Modern technology has done wonders to advance business and give the world a more global perspective. We are repeatedly told we are in the "information age" because the Internet gives us instant access to information on a variety of subjects. In most instances it's a good thing, but I'm not so sure when it comes to dating.

Yesterday, one of my sister-friends and I were talking about a first date she had last week. She is a bit of a celebrity, but not yet a household name. In short, my sister-friend has it going on and her star is rising. She met a guy at a launch event for another friend's new company and they exchanged numbers to set up a date.

In the first few minutes of the date, she realized that he was a little more familiar with her than he should have been. As she was unveiling who she was in the traditional manner it seemed as if he already knew everything she was telling him. Never an arrogant person, she didn't want to assume that he knew who she was, so she asked. No, he wasn't a fan. He had Googled her before their date.

My sister-friend didn't know how to react. The fact that he Googled her made her feel exposed in a way that made her uncomfortable. Typically, she holds back some of her professional information and resume on early dates for a myriad of reasons. First, when a man finds out she's successful and has some fame, then one of two things happen. Either, they become intimidated by it. Or, they fall in love with it before falling in love with her.

I totally get where she's coming from because I've had the same issue on dates. It throws off the dynamic a bit because if there is a lot of information about you online the person has already formed an opinion about you before they get to know the real you. The facts about your life don't make up your complete reality. And, it takes the fun out of a good ole' fashioned 'let's get to know each other' date.

I took an unscientific poll on Twitter and Facebook to see how many people Google a person before a first date. I was shocked to know that more people did than not because I've never done it. One comment I did understand was for safety reasons for women—to make sure the guy wasn't a psycho with a criminal record. I get that reason. Other responses were far less genuinely motivated and underscored my point that it was awkward to Google someone before the first date.

With texting, social media, and the Internet dating has become far less personal than in the past. Personally,

I think some things are best done the old-fashioned way like getting to know a person by talking to them, hanging out, and a series of dates. But it seems I'm in the minority. What do you think, is Googling someone before the first date a good thing?

■ ■ ■

FROM MY SISTER-FRIEND, FLO ANTHONY

My Adorable Friend Nathan Hale Williams - Just thinking about Nathan Hale Williams makes me smile. He is one of the most positive, upbeat people I have ever known. His wonderful spirit is contagious. No matter what challenges he faces, he always has a broad grin on his face that showcases his delicious dimples.

I have known Nathan for over ten years. We first met through mutual friends, when he was producing and starring in Dirty Laundry. However, I got to know him well hanging out at a restaurant, called Native in Harlem. It was our home away from home. We had so much fun.

The best piece of advice Nathan ever gave me was to keep my projects to myself until they materialize and don't tell others, giving them a chance to sabotage your ideas and plans.

He is The Girl's Best Friend because you can confide in him, get good responses, have a wonderful time with him and he understands women. I think that's because he's so close to his mother. He has a respect for women that many men don't have.

I always had so much fun with Nathan. He always comes up with such great ideas and unlike so many others, actually executes them. He is brilliant and very inspiring.

About Flo Anthony—I am a veteran celebrity journalist and bestselling author who hosts a daily syndicated radio feature, "Gossip on The Go with Flo," writes a weekly syndicated column, "Go with The Flo," is a contributor to the Confidential Column in the New York Daily News, and publishes Blacknoir.nyc, an online magazine. I also represent Olympic Gold Medalist, former Light Heavyweight Champion, and Heavyweight Champion of the World, Michael Spinks.

DOES CLASS MATTER?

Over the weekend, I had the extreme pleasure of seeing Alicia Keys' production, *Stick Fly* on Broadway. Lydia R. Diamond's script expertly deals with the cross section of race, culture, and class in our romantic and family relationships. The top-notch, Tony Award worthy performances by Tracie Thoms and Condola Rashad help weave a tale, which demonstrates that even within the black "community" we struggle with issues of class, culture, and social position. It begs the question: "Does class make a difference in dating?"

I always find it ironic when people presume that all black people are the same; we are not. We are as diverse culturally and socially as any other race of people. Often times, our class and socio-economic dynamics are far more complex because of our history of slavery, segregation, and the contemporary separation of the black elite from working class and poor black people. *Stick Fly* evidences all of these nuanced contradictions and led me to think about one of my dear sister-friends.

Five years ago, my sister-friend who is a Managing Director at one of the top investment-banking firms met a plumber. She met him at a picnic. The plumber pursued my sister-friend for weeks and she never returned his calls. Still, she talked about how they'd had an instant connection, how fine he was, and how intelligent he seemed to her.

"Well, why don't you call him back," I remember questioning?

"I can't date a plumber," she quickly replied. I didn't understand why she didn't at least go out with him to see what he was like. Although my sister-friend is no snob, she was confronted by an unsettling dilemma. A well-educated, upwardly mobile, and successful woman dating a blue-collar worker—she couldn't wrap her mind around it.

Just as it happens in the play, my sister-friend had made some assumptions about the plumber that were unfair and inaccurate. True, their economic statuses were on opposite ends of the spectrum. But, that didn't mean that they were culturally different. I encouraged her to call him back and give him a chance. The question really was whether they had similar core values, goals, and life perspectives. I think that upbringing—how someone was raised—is far more important than what they do for a living. As long as he has ambition what does it matter whether his collar is white or blue? Or, does it matter?

Thankfully, she took my advice because five years and two kids later she couldn't be happier. It turned out that the plumber who is now her husband was not just any plumber. Like my sister-friend he was educated and owns a successful business. They enjoyed the same things culturally and had very similar upbringings. He was much closer to her ideal man than the Harvard-educated brokers and lawyers she'd been dating unsuccessfully. And they've learned to cope with the issues surrounding the disparity in their incomes.

Class and socio-economic status do play a major role in all black relationships. We are a complex people. Traditional assumptions may not apply and if you are interested in someone who may (or may not be) from a different class or background it's worth giving it a try. By overcoming your prejudices, you potentially open up your spirit for an unexpected surprise.

(Update: They are still happily married. She is considering leaving the workforce to focus on their children and her artistic interests.)

■ ■ ■

AN INCOMPETENT REPRESENTATIVE

In the hit comedy-concert film, *The Queens of Comedy* comedienne Sommore jokes about men coming with warning labels. She continues to extol about how great it would be if you could read a man's warning labels much like a prescription drug bottle to discover his side effects before dating him. The premise of the joke is that men are rarely completely honest about who they are at the beginning of a relationship.

I agree with Sommore, but I also know that sending a "representative" is something we all do—men and women. It is partly unavoidable due to the nature of dating. Imagine meeting a man and on the first date where he recited a litany of problems and issues spanning from his childhood to now. More than likely, you wouldn't agree to a second date. The question is whether or not the representative you send in those initial stages is a competent one to represent who you really are.

One of my sister-friends is recently engaged and is planning a wedding for next summer. She has been dating her fiancé for almost two years. They do not live together, but spend a great deal of time with one another. She lives in another state and so I had only met him in passing at group functions. However, I never had a chance to sit down and have a real conversation with him.

A few weeks ago, my sister-friend was in town and we were all able to sit down over dinner. Of course, I started sharing my stories about my girl from childhood and college. It's what I do when I meet one of my sister-friend's intended. I could tell she was getting a bit uncomfortable so I pulled back on my anecdotes and jokes. As dinner progressed it became clearer to me that she wasn't acting like herself.

I didn't think too much of it as I chalked it up to the nervous energy when one of your trusted friends meets your significant other; you want them to get along. Then her fiancée brought up the subject of shopping and how he loved the fact that my sister-friend didn't like to shop a lot. Record scratch. "Who? Doesn't like to what," I thought to myself? Clearly, he wasn't talking about her.

For your information, this sister-friend is a notorious shopper and deal hunter. When we were in college her second homes were the library and the mall. When we got our first post-college jobs she went to the *mall every* day. She is very frugal, but she surely loves to shop. For him not to know that was a big deal to me. Red flag!

My sister-friend's fiancée then went on to praise her for her cooking skills, her love of children, and her desire to be a stay at home mother at some point. I almost pinched myself to awake from my dream. As long as I had known her she could not cook, didn't want kids, and was the most ambitious career woman I knew. I know that people change, but she hadn't changed that much. I thought to myself, "who is she fooling?" Needless to say, I kept my mouth shut and went with the flow.

After the dinner we had a moment alone over drinks and I asked her about it. She replied that she'd realized that the woman she had presented to her fiancée was the woman men wanted. She was in her mid-thirties and had been unsuccessful in finding a man to marry being the strong, anti-cooking, and anti-kid woman she truly was. She had acquiesced to become this version. And her validation was the rock on her left hand.

Certainly, I could sympathize with her dilemma. But, I cautioned that the road she was traveling on was a dangerous one. I firmly believe you can only not be yourself for a limited amount of time. You can keep up the guise when you're not around someone 24/7, but what was going to happen when they were married. Over time her honest self and desires were going to surface. And if not, she was going to end up miserable.

The representative my sister-friend had sent was an incompetent one. She definitely had moved on the kids issue and could finally see herself as a mom. And she'd learned how to cook and didn't mind it as much. Notwithstanding the evolution on those two points, being as driven and intelligent as she is I knew she had no real desire to stay at home.

The moment we had over drinks was that moment she'd been dreading. The moment of reckoning that I think she knew deep down would come. I encouraged her to slowly allow some of these points to come up again and discuss with her fiancée. She was far more than a couple of deal points, but it was paramount to the success of their relationship that they got clear.

She's begun to take my advice and talk with her fiancée about some of the things that are important to her. He's been beyond great and understanding. Her approach has been one that I think is loving and open so I think they'll be fine. The good news is that though she had misrepresented some of her beliefs and goals he fundamentally knew the real person.

We all withhold information at the early stages of dating. No one wants to know all the sordid details of your life story on the first date—it's an evolving journey of discovery. But I caution you to make sure that in those early stages (and late ones) of dating you're not sending an incompetent representative.

(Update: This column was a mixture of a couple of different sister-friends. The main sister-friend whose fiancée didn't know she

loved to shop and couldn't really cook has been married over a decade. She still shops, but they can afford her habit and then some. She has become an excellent cook while enjoying being primarily a stay-at-home mom. People do evolve and change.)

■ ■ ■

STOP SIGN UPSIDE THE HEAD

My grandfather's nickname was "Shotgun Gage" when my mother and aunt were growing up on Chicago's south side. "Big Daddy," my term of endearment for him, earned this reputation for the ritual he practiced when guys would come to take out one of his daughters on a date. Big Daddy would put on his cotton short pajamas (so old and thin that they were transparent) and sit in the living room quizzing these gentlemen callers with a rifle laid across his lap.

My mother and aunt were mortified each time this happened and made sure any guy they brought home would pass the test. They'd learned their lessons when guys didn't stack up to Big Daddy's standards. "What alley did you drag this [boy] from?" "You plan on getting a haircut anytime soon, young man?" "Oh, I know your daddy… he ain't [nothing]!" It's funny now considering my mother and aunt married pretty decent men; my mom doing so twice. It reminds me that there used to be a process to dating and the first part of it involved being screened.

Back in the day, men had to court women and that meant meeting their parents especially when they were teenagers and young adults. No man would ask for a woman's hand in marriage without first talking to her family. These days things are different for sure. Some of it is due to changing times and some of it due to our forgetting the value of the family shakedown.

Unfortunately, as young women have become more educated and successful they often move away from their hometowns and are in cities with very little to no family and/or friends. You have to be your own Shotgun Gage. Or, have a close best friend who can play that role for you. More importantly, you have to be very alert of the signs that lead to: this guy is a psycho jerk. They're always there whether you want to recognize them or not.

One of my sister-friends was dating this guy who on paper and on the surface seemed magical. We were all excited for her and all really liked him although none of us really spent that much time around him. Fast forward eight months and I get a distressed call from my sister-friend saying that her bank account was empty and that she had not heard from her "boyfriend" in a week.

She went on to explain that he'd said he needed to get something done to his car, but didn't know how much it was going to cost. "Could she just write him a blank check and he'd hit her back when he got paid?" I know, I know. Sounds like the dumbest thing ever to do, but don't judge her until you've walked a mile. She trusted him. He'd done things for her no other man had done. And we all know love can be a blinding thing.

I am sure I don't have to tell the rest of the story. We're still looking for that brother! I have one mind to post his name on here—or at least the name he gave her. But I won't. In my attempt to help my sister-friend deal with this and move on without blaming herself I asked her to tell me more about their relationship. In the back of my mind, I knew there had been signs along the way to indicate that this dude was not who he said he was.

Sure enough, after she went through the truth about him and their relationship there were stop signs at every turn. She'd hidden from us that he'd moved into her place within two months of dating. She'd been paying his bills. He'd told a tall tale about waiting on some settlement. And the final kicker that she'd found mail with another name on it in his stuff. Stop! Don't do it. Don't judge her. It's easy to Monday night quarterback when you're not in a situation.

For me, the lesson I wanted to impart to her was that she had signs all along and that she should've done some due diligence when the first signs appeared. We're in the Internet Age. Let the World Wide Web be your Shotgun Gage. And don't stop there—have your friends interrogate and ask probing questions. We're often too concerned about overstepping, but which would you rather a pushy friend or an empty bank account?

More importantly, as more single women become remote and isolated from their families you have to be your own Inspector Gadget. Don't take clues lightly. If you feel a certain way about a new man's honesty do your research. I'm not a proponent for searching cell phones or personal email accounts. I am a fan of keeping your eyes open and making sure you're not sleeping with the enemy.

Maya Angelou has one of my favorite quotes, "the first time someone shows you who they are believe them." By simply paying attention and not ignoring signs you will protect yourself from disappointment and potentially danger. By all means, don't let the stop sign hit you upside your head.

■ ■ ■

IT'S THIS ONE THING

Amerie's song lauds the one thing about a potential beau that is driving her crazy in the right way. So much so, it has her "trippin'." We've all been there whether it is the way someone laughs, walks, or speaks that turns us on about that person. Unfortunately, we've all been there when the opposite is true and there's one thing that annoys the hell out of us.

My sister-friend just started dating a guy six weeks ago that she really likes. He is intelligent, worldly, and they have similar interests. He has a great job and is well-established in his career. At thirty-five, he is an anomaly because he has never been married and has no kids. For all intents and purposes, he is an ideal catch except for this one thing. Actually, two in this case—she hates the way he eats and his haircut.

My sister-friend can be a bit persnickety about manners, especially table etiquette. You can imagine the "horror" she encountered when she discovered the guy was no student of Emily Post. She said that she couldn't even enjoy their first dinner because he talked while chewing and chewed loudly. He also has a way of slurping his drink like a Slurpee from the convenience store. At first, I thought she was exaggerating until I went out with them to eat, and she is right there is an issue.

Surprisingly, the lack of table etiquette isn't the biggest deal breaker for her. Homeboy is caught in a bit of a time warp and is still rocking a *somewhat* updated version of the nineties high-top fade. He is a handsome guy and was dressed very nicely the three times I have met him. A real fade would definitely do him a world of good.

My sister-friend was ready to throw in the towel and move on to the next. In our search for perfection, I believe we let some superficial things get in the way of our happiness. I'm certainly not a proponent of the fixer-up man, but correctable attributes like dining habits and haircuts shouldn't be deal breakers. I encouraged her to keep dating him, and then when they get to know each other better attempt to give some helpful suggestions about his etiquette and his haircut. She agreed to try.

With that said, I do have a personal caveat and exception to the above. I once dated someone whose voice raked my nerves like nails on a chalkboard. All other aspects were perfect except that voice. I tried to get over it and ultimately just couldn't. You can change someone's hair, but you definitely can't change someone's voice.

Dating is hard for everyone these days. If you find a potential mate who has that one thing (or two) that gets on your nerves it might be worth it to overlook it if it's something you can work on. If not, it might just be this one thing (that has you steppin').

(Update: It didn't work out with my sister-friend and that guy. Turns out, it was more than his etiquette that annoyed her about him. The etiquette was an indicator of major differences in the way they thought about the world and maneuvered through it. Funniest thing is that the high-top fade made a comeback. I just rocked one for an entire year—the right way.)

■ ■ ■

IS SEX REALLY IMPORTANT?

Actress, Meagan Good recently wed studio executive, DeVon Franklin. Nothing noteworthy about an actress getting married, except the fact the newlyweds made it clear that they were waiting until their wedding night to have sex. It's definitely a changed time because more people thought it was ludicrous than virtuous. It begs the question: In modern times how important is sex?

The wedding sparked a discussion between one of my best sister-friends and a brother-friend regarding the issue of waiting until the wedding night. Surprisingly, my sister-friend was the most adamant about it not being a good idea to wait. In her words: "You wouldn't buy a Mercedes without giving it a test run, sex is too important to a relationship not to know." On the other hand, my brother-friend found it romantic and refreshingly traditional.

We were then joined by another brother-friend who thought it was completely preposterous that they'd waited that long to have intercourse. He didn't believe them. He found it impossible for a man in 2012 not to want to have sex with his fiancé prior to getting married.

Initially, I was on the side of giving your intended a test drive or two before saying I do. But as we talked further, I think Meagan and her new husband might be onto something. I couldn't help, but think of the lyrics of a Mary J. Blige song ("Enough Cryin'"). The lyrics are as follows: "Cause the sex was good you had my mind and I let you back in every time…" Sex can be a major distortion in a relationship both good and bad.

Women were not supposed to openly enjoy sex and weren't socialized to seek quality in a sexual partner like men. Progress rightfully has made women a lot more outspoken and demanding when it comes to sexual pleasure. Hence, why my sister-friend believes in the importance of knowing whether her husband is going to be able to please her in bed.

I get it and agree with the concern, but I presented the scenario of her finding a guy who fit her requirements in all ways except he was a mediocre lover. She said that would be a deal breaker for her. And the vice-verse of a man who was an excellent lover, but lacking in all other areas might get a bit of extra consideration due to his prowess. Her response actually disappointed me a bit because I believe that as important as sex is it is one of the least important ingredients to a long-lasting, fulfilling relationship.

Anyone who has been in a long-term relationship will tell you that (in most cases) the frequency of sex decreases as time and life goes on. Truly important characteristics like compatibility, friendship, sense of humor, mutual respect, trust, and so on can save a relationship when sex can't. Yes, good sex can be the glue that prolongs the inevitable. Good sex rarely can save a failing relationship.

For once in the history of this column, I don't propose to have an answer to my own question. But the discussion with my friends has me thinking about the evolution of our relationships and whether it's for better or worse. I would love to know what you think. Is sex really important in a relationship?

■ ■ ■

FROM MY SISTER-FRIEND, TAI BEAUCHAMP

I remember the day [I met Nathan] vividly but the events that led to that day, I'm not sure. I know we had mutual friends, worked in the same industry, and had crossed paths on several occasions in what is a really a small black entertainment community. But I guess none of that really matters at this point, at least six, maybe seven years later.

For our first one-on-one outing, we agreed to meet in a trendier New York City Flat Iron area restaurant. But it wasn't the food that fed or fueled me. It was our immediate kinship. Most first meetings are somewhat stoic or general where sensible, easy dialogue, and sometimes monologues happen. Not Nathan and me. We shared stories of struggle and triumph. I spoke of my ailing grandmother whom raised me. And how as a thirty-two-year-old caregiver at the time, it felt outer body even after four years of doing so to change the diaper of the woman who bought you your first mink coat for your 16th birthday. He understood and spoke lovingly of his mother who was and is his number one supporter and champion. He spoke of a challenging and heartbreaking breakup and recent health challenges. I spoke of the annoying ass dating scene in NYC, personal and professional goals. We talked about our love of writing...and we prayed.

That for me is always the way you can either create a truly meaningful lifelong connection or not. After and now, we talk about all of the latest things happening in "the industry" or "regular" things and we still pray together. I'm grateful for that.

About Tai Beauchamp—Tai Beauchamp is a veteran journalist and editor with a rare ability to connect with all demographics. Known for her savvy sense of style and ability to deliver inspiring and aspirational insights, women of all ages recognize her as the voice of stylish living. She is also a social entrepreneur and champion for causes, most of them aimed toward youth and education and empowering women through fashion and beauty.

YOU'RE JUST NOT THAT INTO HIM

From the Grammy's to the Oscars, every award ceremony has seat fillers. Seat fillers are people who sit in celebrities' seats while they're gone so there are no empty seats on camera. The problem with seat fillers is that they're just there to take up space and a bit out of place. Far too often I find we date too many seat fillers that we just aren't into.

This weekend I was at brunch with my sister-friend celebrating another friend's birthday. Our love lives came up and I asked her about the guy she'd been seeing for the past three months. She gave a lackluster response about him, which was the norm. He wasn't the most exciting catch in the ocean, but he was a decent guy.

I'd seen how she acted with previous guys and this was definitely not the same. She rarely spoke to him, about him, or brought him around. When she did bring him to a gathering she consistently criticized him and openly worried that he would do something to embarrass her. It was a very uncomfortable situation to see, but he seemed to take it in stride. I often found myself feeling sorry for him although he was grown and able to make his own choices.

So, finally, I asked, "Why are you dating him?" She couldn't give me a good reason beyond the fact that she hated being single, he was nice, and she liked going out to dinner. "That's not a reason to date someone," I responded. "You're wasting your time and his. Clearly, you don't really like him and it's not fair to string him along just to fill space."

She said I was being self-righteous because I'd dated plenty of space fillers in my day. She was right, but that wasn't the point. I know from personal experience that it ended up being a waste of time and I knew early on in the relationship that it wasn't going anywhere. I also know that when I have dated space fillers it has been just so I wouldn't be alone.

The ironic thing is that I made a vow at the beginning of this year not to date anyone else that I'm not really into just for the sake of dating. I realized in doing so I wasn't allowing myself the opportunity to grow personally and I was making myself unavailable for someone who was right for me. It was a bit scary to contemplate because now I'm being forced to deal with my fear of being alone, but it was necessary.

I encouraged my sister-friend to do the same thing. She had plenty of friends to go to dinner with and there was no sense in her continuing to engage with a guy who she didn't like genuinely. I didn't expect that she would act so quickly, but to my surprise she met with him on Monday and broke it off.

Neither one of us can get back the time we spent in dead end relationships (yet, I do believe that every step on your journey is a lesson). We can both make the conscious decision to wait on someone who will start our engines and is what we are looking for in a partner. If you find yourself being ho-hum about the guy you're dating maybe you're just not that into him.

■ ■ ■

HE MIGHT BE WORTH A SECOND DATE

I consistently acknowledge how hard dating can be. It's so difficult that there is an entire industry focused on improving our dating chances. From relationship blogs like this one to matchmakers there are plenty of people out there telling us all how to find love. I think one very simple way to improve your chances is maybe to reconsider giving a not so great first date a second chance.

About a month ago, my sister-friend went out on a disastrous first date. Everything that could go wrong did. First, the guy was thirty minutes late and cited a meeting at work than ran over. He is a lawyer and having practiced in a corporate firm myself that scenario is highly plausible. My sister-friend said the guy said some pretty "foot-in-mouth" things that put her off. If that weren't enough he tipped over the bottle of red wine onto her light-colored dress. She went home shortly after the tragic first date scene in a movie that had come to life.

She was relaying the story to me as a joke with no intention of giving the guy another chance. I asked her some simple questions about the guy in general. Turns out he was an attractive man, who was successful, came from a seemingly good family, never been married, and no kids. On paper he was exactly the kind of man she had been looking to date. But his missteps had turned her off and she no longer saw those qualities.

"You should go out with him again," I said. As you can imagine, she laughed in my face promising that there was no chance in hell. I went on to explain why I thought she should. I think we put too many expectations on a first date. We're all looking for the proverbial spark of love at first sight and when that doesn't happen we get disappointed. First dates are nerve racking and if you're not the smoothest, then those nerves are on full display.

I challenged her to think deeper about it. Was she looking for the smooth talker?" My thought was that her date was nervous and in true form created a comedy of endless errors. I made a deal with her. If she went on another date with him and it was a disaster I would never give her any more advice.

She took the deal and went on a second date—on a Saturday afternoon. The guy was far more relaxed and they got along well. After the horror of the first date she wasn't completely convinced until their third date. They've been dating since then and having a great time. I'm definitely a friend that will say, "I told you so," and I did. I was happier that my gamble paid off for her.

In the precarious world of modern dating the first date may not be the best indicator of someone. If you find yourself on a comically tragic date, but with someone who seems pretty decent, he might be worth a second date.

■ ■ ■

A MATTER OF REJECTION

The singular most universal impediment to dating is the fear of rejection. It is the four-letter word of dating. We've all experienced it, which is why we all fear it on some level. It is the most awful feeling to be into someone to discover they're just not that into you.

Just the other day, one of my most special sister-friends and I were out having cocktails (a typical exercise for us). I'm fortunate because most of my sister-friends are pretty amazing. But she is even that much more amazing. She's not just pretty, she's striking, owns her own business, the life of the party, and down-to-earth. If I'm traveling, I want her to be my companion. To call her an "It Girl" would be an understatement. Yes, she's *all* that!

Tooting her horns aside, my sister-friend and I were out talking about work, and of course our love lives. She had just been on several dates with this guy she'd met on an online dating service. Although she'd met some guys who had the credentials she was looking for none of them sparked her interest like this guy had. Even with her excitement she was cautious because he hadn't initiated contact in a couple of days.

"It's funny because I went to [match-making site] and it said, he'd checked out my profile yesterday," she said. But he had not called her. She was starting to feel a bit uneasy because in her theory when someone is into you they correspond every day in the beginning. Not a bad theory so I wasn't going to argue. And then her phone rang. It was the guy.

After giving me the look, I said, "Take the call girl! Plus, I'm nosy." She stepped away for a few minutes and came back with a forlorn look on her face. I immediately asked what happened. The guy told her that it wasn't working for him and he thought enough of her to let her know directly. As she slumped back into her seat, I raised my hand for the waiter; it was clearly time for some Patron shots.

"Why is it that the ones that are into it, aren't 'it'? And the ones you're into never seem to work out," my sister-friend pitifully questioned.

I replied, "Because we can't be everyone's type, no matter how fabulous we are." I explained that just as those guys that were into her (and there were a countless number) didn't spark her fancy in the right way; she wasn't going to be right for everyone she liked.

"Don't let this rejection sting you too long girl. *Everyone* gets rejected. It's not a measure of you as a woman. Probably just a matter of preference." Now, that was my practical answer. Then I told her what was on my heart and probably the truth. "Most guys don't know what they want. You're probably too much for him and it's a good thing you found out now. Any guy that doesn't see the dime that you are and all of the love you have in you, then he's not worth your time nor is he right for you. Thank him! He did you a favor."

Ironically, my sister-friend had just been on a journey of self-discovery and spiritual awakening. She was in a great place in her life and very happy. Encouraging her, I said, "The moment you had with him just continues to affirm that you're open to love. You are getting closer to 'him' and you can't let this get you down."

My sister-friend sat there for a minute, and then her winning spirit kicked in. "You're right! I did get excited because he was closer to what I've been looking for, but if I'm honest he wasn't completely it…he was too damn short," she joked. Through laughter I could tell her work on her own spirit and self-esteem had paid off in gold. She was genuinely able to bounce back in about fifteen minutes. And when she got back home she jumped back on the dating site to set-up another date.

The fear of rejection can be a single-person's kryptonite. Too often we take rejection at more than face value—as an indictment or critique of who we are. In fact, it's not really a negative thing. Someone is doing you a favor by not wasting your time when they have no interest in establishing something meaningful with you. If you find yourself being rejected don't make it more than what it is and take it personally. He was probably too short anyway.

■ ■ ■

DATING MULTIPLE MEN

Not too long ago a brother from Texas called me out in one of his comments on *Essence.com*. He accused me of being another black man selling out guys to make a "buck" off of women. The comment didn't offend me because it couldn't be further from the truth or my mission. I think the crux of his frustration is that I often call out the double standards for women in relationship to men. One of those double standards is the ability to date multiple people at once.

A recently divorced sister-friend and I were talking about how excited she was to finally jump back into the dating scene. She survived a very long separation and subsequent divorce. During which time she was focused on healing and dealing with the emotional strain of that drama. She wanted her spirit to be clear before entering into a new relationship and I supported her in that decision. She is ready now to get her groove back and I completely support that one too.

Being the fly girl she is, it didn't take my sister-friend long to go on her first few dates. Actually, she had four dates in one week. She was in overdrive and loving it. At first, she was concerned about being rusty, but in her words, it was "like riding a bike." She fell back into the swing of things despite a ten-year hiatus. I congratulated her because that is rare for most people.

My sister-friend then said to me, "But, I have a major problem." I asked her what could be the problem since she was having so much success. "I like them all," she replied. I fell out laughing because who would ever think that a perfect batting average could be a problem. She went onto explain that she had never dated multiple guys at once. "I don't want people thinking I'm [loose]!"

Her comment led to a discussion about the double standard for men and women in dating. Men can date as many girls as they want and are viewed as playboys or players. Women on the other hand are viewed less favorably and given not so nice titles. It's a long talked about issue, but even in this day my sister-friend was concerned about it, which means the double standard still exists.

"Well, if you like them all, then date them all. Be upfront with them that you're not looking for anything serious or even monogamous if that's the case. And if they can't deal that'll make room for another one," I said encouraging her. The last thing she needed was to jump back into a serious relationship with someone before she determined what was out there swimming around in the sea.

I knew the reality was that many guys weren't going to be able to deal with a woman being so candid about dating other guys although men do it all the time. But she couldn't be worried about what the guys thought or anyone else for that matter. It's a different time so I further encouraged her to enjoy it and focus only on what she wanted. It was time she started living for herself by her standards.

We all are challenged by society's concept of what is right or wrong. It can handcuff your life if you live by someone else's standards especially in dating. If you have it like that, why not date multiple men? I say, play on "Playette."

■ ■ ■

A TRIP TO COUGAR TOWN

My mother called me one day a couple of years back with a sullen voice of shame. She had something to tell me. "Last night I had a dream about a man," she said. Clearly, I didn't see the problem with it and was quite happy. "He's a much younger man." Still, I couldn't see the issue. She said, "The young man was Usher. Would you mind if I ever dated a younger man?" After controlling my laughter, I assured her I would not especially if it were Usher.

Recently, one of my sister-friends came to me with a similar real-life dilemma. She'd met a man on one of the popular dating sites, but he was thirteen years her junior. She'd gone on a date with him and was very interested. Yet, she couldn't get over his age. "He's the same age as [her younger brother] that's gross," she said.

"But sweetheart he's not your brother," I replied. I'm always for an expansive view on dating and love so I really didn't see the problem. If the man was mature, made her happy, and could hold his own, then his age really shouldn't matter. We all know plenty of "forty-some things" that act their shoe size and not their age.

From what she described the guy had his life together. A great job. No kids. Good family background. And by her account, he was fine as hell. My only caveat was that although he might be mature on paper and in first impression if she were to enter a long-term relationship with him she would have to always take his age into consideration when judging his actions.

"But you just said his age shouldn't matter," she questioned confused? True, but having been in a relationship with someone who was ten years my senior I also knew there were some considerations. At twenty-six years old, I was a successful lawyer and had my act together too. But, I was still twenty-six when I entered into the relationship. And often my partner assumed I was mature enough to make certain decisions that in fact I was not. I hadn't lived enough and experienced enough to process life on his level.

Ultimately, I was mature professionally, but not so much personally. I'd devoted my entire life to achieving in school and work. In my personal life, I was very much a twenty-something that was still wet behind the ears. I gave my sister-friend some examples of how that came up in my relationship and the issues it caused. Notwithstanding the undeniable generalities that come with age, every person is different and my experience wasn't necessarily the rule.

I encouraged my sister-friend to explore the relationship with him. They've been out on more dates and it has continued to go well. In my opinion, she had nothing to lose and everything to gain. And a little young love might put a pep in her step.

I consistently say that dating is hard for everyone. The more restrictions you put on your potential partner shrinks your dating pool. Therefore, if a young tender catches your eye don't be so quick to throw the Guppy back in the ocean he might be just what you need.

■ ■ ■

LONG DISTANCE LOVE

Due to technology modern relationships are quite different than in the past. In many instances technology has made it easier to stay in touch with loved ones. For instance, I talk to my Godchildren regularly via Skype. I do believe that technology has played a part in diminishing true interpersonal contact and skills. One thing that technology has made easier is a long-distance relationship, but would you be in one?

Ironically, two of my sister-friends are confronted with the possibility of long distance relationships yet under distinct scenarios. My first sister-friend has been casually dating a guy for a couple of months that currently lives in the same city. They'd resisted dating and had remained distant because the guy knew he might be relocating. Still, they couldn't fight their attraction and despite their efforts to keep it friendly began to date.

My other sister-friend was on a business trip and went out with a guy she'd met through a mutual friend years ago. They'd been Facebook friends for some time and had occasionally exchanged messages. They went out and hit it off ultimately going out every day that she was in town.

I'm not opposed to long distance relationships in theory. I've been in one successful one before that lasted three years. In the end, it wasn't the distance that was the issue, but fundamental personality issues. Thus, I do believe that long distance relationships can work depending on a few factors.

First, I think it is easier to have a long-distance relationship with someone who has once lived in the same city as you. In a weekend romance, it is hard to determine those key day-to-day elements that can make or break a relationship. The distance might prove to be a benefit for two busy schedules who would be pressured if they lived in the same city. I also do think that you can't truly get to know someone from afar—modern technology or not.

Resources also play a major role. If two people have the resources and time to see each other it makes the odds of a long-distance relationship succeeding much better. There is no technology that will take the place of direct human contact. Intimacy is a fundamental ingredient to a healthy relationship.

Finally, I think there has to be some end point in sight. One of the parties has to be open to the possibility of relocating. To me, this is the trickiest part because I firmly believe that a person should not relocate solely for someone else. There has to be a desire to live in the new city or you're opening up Pandora's Box especially if it doesn't work out.

I gave them both the same advice. These days it's very difficult to find someone you want to date in the first place. So why not go for it. The worst thing that could happen is that it doesn't work out. It's the same with any dating scenario. It makes no sense to close off a potentially great future just because of geography.

I think there are three factors in determining whether a long-distance relationship has a chance. But I know many people who as a rule will not entertain a long-distance relationship. What about you, would you date long distance?

■ ■ ■

BE A PRIORITY, NOT AN OPTION

My friend, celebrity blogger and personality, B.Scott tweeted this yesterday, "If you spend too long holding on to the one who treats you like an option, [you] will miss finding someone who treats you like a priority." It was so on time that I told him I had to write about it. A simple concept, but time and time again I see many of my friends settling for the role of the option.

The Twitter quote took me back about a year when I was sitting at lunch with one of my sister-friends. She is an awesome person, but has always felt "average." In a city like New York that is full of exceptional people it can be even more profound if you've always felt like someone in the middle. I get it. I think she's wrong about herself, but still I understand.

She'd been dating this guy for a year when we had our lunch last year. Dating is difficult everywhere. In New

York City, multiply the level of difficulty times ten. For this reason, my sister-friend was happy to be dating a man with a solid job, handsome enough, and who had all of his teeth. Yes, it's that hard in the Big Apple. I could sense though that she wasn't completely happy.

"Where do you see the relationship going? Have you all talked about marriage yet?" I asked. She shook her head, "No." I asked if she even saw herself marrying him.

"We've never discussed it. Every time I bring it up he changes the subject and says not to push him," she replied sadly. Red flag! First, her reaction to my question told me more than her words. Secondly, I truly believe that the great majority of men who've found their wife know within the first year and begin to discuss marriage pretty quickly.

I must have opened Pandora's Box because she started spilling her frustrated guts. Basically, the guy was typically unresponsive to she and her needs. They'd stopped actually going out on dates about six months into the relationship. She would cook for him. He would come over to her house. They would have sex. He would leave in the morning. Repeat. And he broke the cardinal rule (well, she let him). He would consistently call the day of and sometimes the evening of when he wanted to "chill" with her.

"If someone is calling you the day of to make plans with you rest assured you are just an option," I said. A year into the relationship this shouldn't have been happening. If he couldn't keep up the courting and romance for a year, then there was no hope for the future. And if there's no hope for the future there was really no point. My sister-friend heard me, however, I could tell she didn't *hear* me.

It made me sad because I could sense the fear and helplessness she felt. It was becoming that hard for an intelligent black woman to find a man. And for all intent and purpose, this guy was a "good man." But just because he was a "good man" didn't mean he was good for her. Moreover, she clearly was not a priority in his life and there probably wasn't anything she could do to change it. I told her to let him go.

"Easier said than done! As much as I want more, I definitely don't want to be lonely every night. I want *somebody* in my life, "she explained.

I retorted, "So you'll just settle for any ole' thing to have *some* body?" I went on to explain that while she was settling for option status there was a guy out there waiting to upgrade her. Sticking around with this guy because he was *some*body might just be blocking her from the man that was to be her true blessing.

My sister-friend continued to date the dude for a couple more months. Fast forward to last week (after about nine months since our last meeting) and we met to catch-up and gossip. Plus, she had some great news for me—she was engaged. I knew she'd been dating a new guy who by all of our friends' accounts was terrific. "You were a hundred percent correct! I was so desperate for a man that I'd allowed myself to take a backseat position." And she went on to describe the difference with her fiancé. He made her a priority in every sense of the word. She was completely happy and excited.

We've all been there—dating someone who has not made you a priority in their life. Don't let the difficulty of dating allow you to settle for less than you deserve. We deserve to be in the pole position in our lover's life. Wasting your time on someone who does not put you in that place may be getting in the way of you finding someone who will. Just say to yourself, I deserve to be a priority not an option.

■ ■ ■

FROM MY SISTER-FRIEND, MEYAKO HUGHES

"You attract the energy that you put out." Some of the best advice I have ever needed and received to get me through a tough time. But like most advice, we often take it and promise to remember it forever, but life happens, and you forget. That is why I am so grateful to have Nathan Hale Williams as my family and friend... always here to remind me.

Nathan has been a blessing in my life for over twenty-three years. We met during my freshman year at University of Illinois-Urbana-Champaign through what would become sharing Danielle Walker, our best friend. Danielle lived next door to me and while coming home from class one day, I saw a young man dancing to "Cherchez La Femme" from the hall into Danielle's room. I had to see whom this fabulous person was and that I did... life has never been the same.

The fabulous times we have shared cannot be compared or replaced with anything else. There are too many to count, but one that still brings me to tears involved lots of libations and my first spades game at U of I (or ever for that matter). Nathan was paired with Danielle, as was the norm, and I was paired with one of our other close sister friends. During the game, I was already nervous, and in that tension, I mistakenly told them I was out of a particular card suit, not realizing I had it. Later, I played that exact suit. Well, Nathan screamed to the top of his lungs "Renege! Renege! Renege!" and on that third scream fell out of his chair. His first words were not "ouch" it was, "Is my drink ok? I just poured that!"

In true Nathan fashion, he pulled himself together, sat down, took a sip of his drink and looked at me and said you still, "Reneged." We all fell out laughing. That day I learned how to play spades and never misplayed my hand again. I can go on and on with more fabulous stories from college: fashion show foolery to my visits to see him and Danielle in Philly. Recounting my times with Nathan still makes me laugh out loud and smile with pride.

I can say, without a doubt, that Nathan has been my date, advisor, muscle, family, shoulder, and comedian. I would not trade it ever. That makes him "The Girl's Best Friend." Even with his amazing knack for always having the right words for any situation, he has a heart of gold. That heart has always given me the best advice for any of my messy life situations. The best part is that he has always given me a man's perspective while uplifting me. So that quote from him, "You attract the energy that you put out," is the best. If the energy I put out brings me great friendships like Nathan, then I am on the right track.

About Meyako Hughes—I was born and raised in Chicago, Illinois. As I stated earlier, I graduated from University of Illinois-Urbana-Champaign in 1998 with a degree in Communications. In recent years I spent time working in Miami, but had to return to my true love Chicago. I have spent a large part of my professional life consulting in the areas of technology and media. My side passions are fashion, virgin seamstress, photography and reading anything informative and fun. Life has given me many ups and downs, but my faith, family, friendship, and a hopeful heart have kept things exciting to say the least.

LESSONS FROM MISS PIGGY

It was so good to see one of my favorite actresses featured at this year's Oscars, Ms. Piggy. Since childhood, I have adored the Muppets and Ms. Piggy has always been my favorite. It makes so much sense to me now. Like many of my sister-friends, she is fabulous, successful, and a no-nonsense diva. Ms. Piggy was the original "independent woman," but still don't mess with her man, Kermy.

I was having cocktails with one of my sister-friends and she was annoyed that her boyfriend said she was too nonchalant about their relationship. According to him, it felt like she could take him or leave him. She thought he was being silly and overly sensitive. And she told him so.

"Players need love too," I said to her half joking. My friend is the ultimate modern woman and things that tend to affect other women don't bother her at all. She doesn't get flustered when women flirt with him, if he stays out too late, or if they miss a day of texting/calling. Seemingly, my sister-friend is a man's dream.

I told her that she needed to take some notes from Ms. Piggy and step up her game. At times to an extreme, it is always clear to Kermit where Ms. Piggy stands in regard to their relationship. He is her man—end of story. In a recent commercial, she karate chopped googly-eyed Vanessa L. Williams in the back declaring, "That's my frog…desperate hussy." Ms. Piggy was not having it.

I pulled up the commercial on You Tube; and after we stopped laughing uncontrollably, I explained my point. True, men often complain about the overbearing, controlling, and distrustful girlfriend. My sister-friend, however, had taken it too far. Her laissez-faire attitude made him feel unwanted, unprotected, and undesired. Three adjectives that no man ever wants to feel from his woman.

"Men, kill me. They want it all. I can't tell you how many guys I've dated who have treated me the exact same way. Over time I realized that since I couldn't beat them I might as well join them," she proclaimed. And she was right. Women complain about feeling those same three adjectives far more often than men do. The thing missing in both scenarios is balance.

"I'm not saying you "piggy chop" every chick that looks at [her boyfriend], but showing a little interest (aka jealousy) will go a long way." Everyone wants to feel appreciated in relationships and some times that means putting up a little fight even it is playful. If you don't it gives the impression that you don't care. I get it. Thankfully, she got it too. And it worked. She paid a little more attention and he appreciated it.

Modern times present a conundrum of dilemmas for relationships. No one wants to be in a relationship with a jealous dictator. The same is true for someone who can care the least about what you do or with whom you do it. We can all learn a couple of lessons from Ms. Piggy.

■ ■ ■

HE'S NOT CHANGING

One slow Saturday I was watching one of "those" shows. You know the shows intelligent people hate to admit they watch, but I was bored and nothing else was on television. The show was, "Love & Hip-Hop," and one woman was telling the other woman (I really don't know their names) that she should hang in there with the rapper guy she was dating (I think Fabolous) because he would eventually change. I immediately turned the television to the Food Network. Bored or not I couldn't take any more.

Ironically, I've heard this same "wisdom" given to one of my sister-friends who was dating a basketball player. After a string of discovered infidelities, one of her so-called friends told her that she should basically suck it up because he was going to eventually stop playing basketball, stop being on the road, and then settle down to be faithful. I couldn't disagree more.

As I told my sister-friend, it is illogical and unfair for someone to wait for a change in his or her partner's repeated bad behavior. First, it sends the wrong message that bad behavior is acceptable if you know the other person will grow up and do the right thing. Secondly, it says that the person waiting on this change is somehow inferior or desperate and needs to wait. Lastly, it takes the burden off of the perpetrator and places it on the victim.

More importantly, you could easily find yourself waiting for years and this presumed change never comes. I encouraged my sister-friend not to put her life on hold and demand that she be treated the way she deserved to be treated right now. Tomorrow is not promised. And suffering today for an uncertain tomorrow is not good living. If your partner can't live up to your expectations and conduct himself or herself properly today, then you probably need to change partners.

You would never hear a guy telling another guy, "hang in there dawg she'll grow out of it and get tired of cheating on you." Never going to happen. It baffles me that women give this advice to each other about sticking it out when the men in their lives consistently fail them.

It goes straight to the imbalance in our society between women and men. Unfortunately, I believe women are socialized to think that they are less than without a man. No matter how successful, happy, or fulfilled they are in their single lives if they don't have a man something is wrong. It causes women to put up with and let men get away with things that are completely unacceptable. But it's up to women to change that imbalance and demand a certain standard from the men in their lives.

Certainly, there will be no shift in the inequality if women keep sticking it out hoping a no-good guy is going to somehow miraculously make a shift. Truly, the only person you can change is you. I think you should reevaluate your position in a relationship if you find yourself saying, "I'll hang in there, he'll change."

■ ■ ■

A CIVIL BREAKUP

During his [first] presidential campaign, President Obama said that he would seek to restore civility to Washington, D.C. If the last few weeks are any indication his efforts may have been in vain. It's not just from the politicians in the capitol that we need more civility; we need more civility in all of our relationships. Most importantly, when that relationship is coming to an end.

Two of my sister-friends are experiencing break-ups. For one, a romantic relationship is ending and the other a friendship. Ironically, the long-term relationship is ending civilly. My other sister-friend's friendship is not. And it's all because of the way in which the people have chosen to act in each situation.

My first sister-friend has been in a relationship for about eight years. She met her boyfriend when she was twenty-four and he was thirty-eight. They had a remarkable relationship during which both of them grew professionally and in prominence. To most people, they were an ideal couple and many people looked up to them.

One of the things that was most remarkable about their relationship was the way in which they treated each other. You would never catch them in a disagreement publicly or bad mouthing each other, or anything of the sort. They always regarded each other with respect and allowed the other their dignity. They always acted civilly towards each other. And from what my sister-friend says that's how they were in private as well.

Throughout the course of their relationship my sister-friend changed as he matured. Her needs and wants from a partner changed as well. Her boyfriend fulfilled her when she was younger, but she was no longer in the same space. They tried for the last two years to make it work and it just didn't. Finally, she decided to move out and he agreed that was the best thing.

He wished her well and tearfully helped her move into her new place. Both of them have nothing, but good things to say about each other and deeply cherish their years together. As with all relationships there were bad times, arguments, some infidelity, but they've chosen to focus on the good in the relationship and in each other. By doing so they've been able to have a civil and amicable break-up and will undoubtedly remain friendly.

My other sister-friend is experiencing something completely different in her break-up with her friend. A girl friend of hers recently just stopped talking to her without warning or reason. Although my sister-friend wouldn't have considered her one of her best friends they did hang out a lot. They were definitely road dogs.

At first, my sister-friend didn't understand what was going on between them. They'd almost instantaneously gone from speaking ten times per day to not communicating at all. My sister-friend would call and have her call returned via e-mail or text if at all. She reached out to her friend to see if they could get together and talk. No response. It was clear she was being completely shut out and she had no idea why.

She then started hearing things from their mutual friends and basically her friend was going around spreading the rumor that my sister-friend was a social climber who had been using [the friend] for years. My sister-friend was devastated and started "setting the record straight" and retaliating with her own harsh words.

It all devolved into a big she say/she say mess with daggers being thrown from both sides. It became an all-out war between my sister-friend and her friend. She was distraught over the situation because any war will tax the warrior's emotions. She asked me what she should do.

The core problem was a lack of communication between she and her friend. They'd allowed themselves to be involved in a game of mean girl telephone that had gotten out of hand. Had her friend addressed her issues directly with my sister-friend it probably would've been avoided. But because she did not act civilly it turned into chaos.

I told my sister-friend that she had the power to end it by extending an olive branch. She should apologize for her bad acts, own them, and forgive herself as well as her friend. Even if they were going to end their relationship they could do it with dignity and civility. At first this was hard for my sister-friend to digest after all that had been said—she was hurt. But she fortunately took my advice and reached out.

Unfortunately, her friend never responded, but that's on her. By acting civilly and doing the right thing it took the burden off of my friend and she was freed from the drama. The lesson she learned is one I learned a while back that no matter what someone else does if you conduct yourself in a civil manner there's no way for it to turn into a mess. She felt good and has been able to move on.

People enter your life for a reason, season, or a lifetime. If it's for a season and that season is coming to an end you both have a choice on how you will handle the break-up. I truly believe how someone leaves your life will determine whether or not they re-enter it. No matter what has previously transpired you should choose civility.

■ ■ ■

THANK MR. WRONG

One of the biggest obstacles to having a good dating life is trying to fit a square peg into a hole. All too often I see both women and men attempting to make a relationship work that is just not meant to be. I see many of my sister-friends getting down when that relationship doesn't work out. Instead, I think they should be thanking "Mr. Wrong" because he made room for "Mr. Right."

Case in point is one my dear sister-friends was dating a guy in the fall of 2011. A blind man could see that they weren't right for each. Physically the guy was extremely attractive, but his attributes stopped there. He was boring, not so bright, and lacked a sense of humor. On the contrary, my sister-friend has an ebullient personality and is highly intelligent. Talking to her is like a sunny day while talking to him was like watching paint dry.

Following her inevitable break-up from "Mr. Hell No" she was sad for almost three weeks. Instead of coddling her, I laughed at her and scolded her because she wasn't really missing anything more than the idea of having a man—wrong or not. She then followed him with a string of guys that showed little to no interest in her by evidence of their word and actions. To my sister-friend's credit, describing it sounds much worse than it actually was, but it was baffling for me because she is an outstanding woman.

A month ago, we met up for drinks and she brought with her the new guy she had been dating. I was skeptical and so I dreaded meeting yet another one of her "M.W.'s." To my surprise it was love at first sight…for me. He was an exceptional human being, attractive, smart, witty, and all of those laundry list of things you look for in a partner. More importantly, he was clearly into her and she was visibly into him.

We ended up hanging out all night and I thoroughly enjoyed not only being around him, but around them as a couple. It seemed to click in the way relationships should. We've all been around those two people that seem to be meant for each other and we've been around those two people who should never speak again. It is why I don't understand why we can't tell the difference in our own love lives.

Last week, she called and said those four words, "I found Mr. Right." The honeymoon had continued. And after seeing them together I believed her. I'm so happy for her and I have a feeling it's just going to get better. They're already talking about marriage, which is a good sign from a guy. I always say if a guy wants to marry you he will talk about it rather quickly.

Those string of bad relationships that didn't work out were a blessing to my sister-friend. Had she been stuck in those dead-end relationships the ending of which seemed catastrophic at the time she'd never met her "M.R." The next time a bad relationship ends make sure you thank Mr. Wrong (and keep it moving toward Mr. Right).

(Update: Their whirlwind relationship continues to this day. They got married pretty quickly after they started dating. They have a young son and nothing has changed from my initial impression. I have grown to love her husband even more than when I first met him. Yay!)

■ ■ ■

CREATE NEW OPPORTUNITIES

Albert Einstein said, "The definition of insanity is doing the same thing over and over again and expecting different results." We all have habits or patterns in our lives that we know do not yield the best fruit, but we keep doing the habits anyway. I believe it stems from fear of the unknown. In order to get different results, we must do things differently and create new opportunities for ourselves.

One of my favorite songs to play for someone's birthday is 50 Cents', "In Da' Club." I also like Beyoncé's remix. By all accounts, 50's version is a hot song. It made him a hit rapper. And it lets you know where you can find him… in the club.

Whenever I hear the song it reminds me of one of my sister-friends. She has the most party ready personality—always happy and always in the club. Pick a day of the week and your best bet would be that she's somewhere getting her drink on and kicking it. I don't judge her because she is young, single, handles her business professionally, and just a damn good person. And she's no "loosey goosey." She simply likes to have fun.

After the New Year, my sister-friend decided she wanted to make some changes. She was trying to figure out why she'd been unlucky in love. She had no problem meeting guys. They approached her all the time. She was knocking on thirty's door and was starting to crave a stable relationship with a man. Unfortunately, all the guys she was dating were looking to have casual relationships. She had been fine with this in past as she focused most of her attention on building her career. Things were changing and she wanted more.

I asked my sister-friend, "Where do you meet most of the guys you date?" You know what she said…in the club. No wonder. I am not knocking meeting people in the club, but your chances of meeting "Mr. Right" in the club are not the greatest. I do know some married folks with great relationships who met in the club. My best friend met her husband in the club. Although for the most part, the relationships that I know of that started in the club didn't last.

My sister-friend being the sassy diva she is replied, "where else am I going to meet guys? I'm always at the club." She made my point for me. I argued that if she repeatedly failed to meet the type of guys she was looking for at the club why was she always there. I told her that she needed to create new opportunities for herself.

"You sound like Dr. Phil," my sister-friend replied. We both laughed as I went to explain what I meant. The club is fun, but what about a trip to a museum. She used to be active in softball in college. Try joining a co-ed softball league. I'm not one for going to church solely to meet a husband or a wife, but if it happens it's certainly not a bad place to meet someone. Of course, she couldn't remember the last time she'd been to a museum (or to church). I continued down a laundry list of places and activities where she could potentially meet the caliber of men she was looking for now.

It's hard to teach an old dog new tricks and so at first my sister-friend disregarded my advice. Instead, she decided to go back with an ex-boyfriend she'd been dating off and on for about seven years. It takes a lot to upset me, but that pissed me off. She was doing the exact opposite of what I advised. My advice is no golden rule, but I thought it was pretty solid in this circumstance and she completely ignored me.

I had reached the conclusion that my sister-friend was insane. If it has never worked out in the seven years you've been trying this it is not going to miraculously work out this time. It didn't. Last week over dinner she came crying back to me. She and the guy went down the same path they always did ending in disaster. Thankfully, it made her ready to try some new things and do some things differently.

It's only been a week, but we're scheduling some new events on her agenda. I'll let you know how it goes. I am certain that she is going to see a difference in the men she meets outside of the club.

We all have habits that are hard to break especially when it comes to dating and relationships. If you find your habits are yielding the same unwanted results maybe it's time to break those patterns and create some new opportunities for yourself.

(Update: She met a man in the club and they've been dating ever since I wrote this column. I still stand by my advice. This particular sister-friend has a different set of relationship goals than most. It turns out that she prefers to keep it at the boyfriend level as she has realized she does not want to get married or have kids. She and her man kick it together all of the time…hard. You can find them in the club.)

∎ ∎ ∎

DUST YOURSELF OFF
AND TRY AGAIN

"For me, it's God and then family! I thank God for choosing me to receive the gift of you wife!! I Love You! As real men we are given the responsibility to take care of our family. I am clocked in and my time sheet is [submitted].... Hallelujah!"

The statement above is what one of my newly married sister-friend's husband wrote on her wall on Facebook. It struck such a strong chord with me for many reasons and on many levels. It was a wonderful thing for him to say to her about his commitment to their family. It also confirmed my belief that you should never give up on love.

My sister-friend is a dynamic and fabulous woman in her mid-thirties. She's gorgeous, successful, smart, down-to-earth, loving, and has one of the most generous spirits that I know. Before now she hadn't enjoyed the best of luck in love. She'd been previously married and after her divorce a string of unfortunate relationships followed. I didn't understand it because she is awesome.

Despite having been repeatedly disappointed by men my sister-friend never gave up. Nor did she become bitter or jaded. Relationships wouldn't work out, but she'd get right back in the saddle and go for it again. I admired that about her because she was resilient and determined.

When she first met her new husband, all of our friends were concerned, yet hopeful. I remember being on our annual vacation weekend and she told me, "This is the one!" Having not met her boyfriend I was admittedly skeptical. But there was a new confidence in her about this relationship and this man that hadn't been there before. I got excited for her.

My sister-friend started telling us stories of: how he treated her; the things he said to her; and, his general philosophy on life and love. I got even more excited! Finally, she was being shown the love and treatment that I knew she deserved all along. I remember praying for her that this would continue and this guy would keep up the good work. Well, he did! They were married last month in a beautiful island ceremony.

I learned such a valuable lesson from my sister-friend's story and I hope you can too. She could have easily thrown in the towel and become resolved to the general perception that there are no "good men" left. Instead, she decided to rely on her faith that God wanted her to be happy and would send her the right man in due time. Her determination and faith kept her focused.

My sister-friend never lowered her standards just to get or keep a man. She had an expectation of what her man should be and she stuck with it. If guys didn't live up to those expectations she moved on. She never allowed herself to go down to a man's level that was not up to par. She'd given plenty of men who weren't quite there an opportunity to elevate their game. When they didn't rise to the occasion she was strong enough to let the relationship go.

I am happy for her and her new husband. Her journey epitomizes all of the things I believe in about love and that I write about in this column: 1) faith that true love exists and is out there waiting for you; 2) maintaining your standards and never settling; 3) remaining optimistic and hopeful; and, 4) working on self to be prepared when that real love comes.

As we get older it is easy to become cynical especially when it comes to relationships. And particularly when you have had several bad ones. But if finding love is your goal you can never be deterred from searching for it. A string of relationships may not work out, but you cannot give up. Instead, be like my sister-friend get back up dust yourself off and try again.

(Update: Uggh! I hate to tell you that they ultimately divorced. I'll save the details to protect my sister-friend's privacy. But I will say that she remains resilient and has dusted herself off and trying again.)

■ ■ ■

DON'T STOP LOOKING

A few years ago, *The Secret* was all the rage. Oprah had the author and many of the various figures in the book on her show to discuss the best-selling phenomenon. *The Secret* came out at a time when I was searching for some answers so I decided to read it. The most important thing I learned from *The Secret* is its main premise: you attract the energy you put out.

Although *The Secret* didn't fully satisfy my longings for clarity, I did learn that you must have intention behind your goals and the life you've imagined. I don't agree that all you have to do is envision something and it will happen. I do know that you must believe that it will happen. Contrary to some schools of thought I think the same is true with dating and relationships.

Last week, one of my single sister-friends and I were talking about this whole notion that you should stop looking for a significant other. It has been three years since she was in a committed relationship and she hadn't been dating a lot. It was mostly by choice as she is a great, gorgeous woman with a lot to offer. But she had heard all of these relationship advice experts tell her that she shouldn't be looking for a boyfriend.

We began this discussion about this concept that perplexed us both. We understood the underlying argument—focus on making yourself better and if you do that the mate will come. The reason why this doesn't ring completely true is that little thing I learned from *The Secret* about putting energy and intention behind your goals. It seemed impossible to find something for which you weren't looking.

To both of us, it seemed so unnatural to "stop looking." Why would you stop looking if being in a relationship is one of your goals? We all know that when a relationship is a desire and priority every eligible (and some ineligible) person that you encounter and are attracted to raises a thought in your mind. It's natural and automatic.

As we discussed this further, I realized why that line of advice misses the point. First, I truly believe you must connect energy and action with your goals. Second, it is unnatural to completely shut yourself off when meeting new people and not helpful to the process of finding someone. Third, it presupposes that one can't work on self and find love at the same time. And finally, I think it confuses "looking" for being "thirsty."

My guru (in my head), Ms. Oprah Winfrey is always telling us that for anything to happen in your life you must first believe it will. Subconsciously, we all know that to be nothing, but the truth. Unfortunately, we feed ourselves such bad information about ourselves that we use the power of that truth in the wrong direction. Instead of believing in positive, self-affirming things we accept the opposite into our spirit.

If you have a list of attributes, qualifications, and so on that you're looking for in a man, then you must believe that he exists and that you will find him. Even if you're more flexible and just want to find true love you must believe that will happen for you. You must put intention (belief) behind your goals and actions. If you're actively taking inaction (*i.e.* not looking) it doesn't synergize with you believing and putting intention behind your goals.

I don't know about you, but when I meet single, eligible people that I'm attracted to the thought always goes through my mind, "Could this be the one?" But if I were in the mode of "not looking," then I wouldn't even entertain that thought. I don't think that's possible or healthy. I wrote a column about remaining open and how essential it is to finding love. Whenever you put the word stop in a sentence it is a period. The end. Not a good look if love is your goal.

Finally, my sister-friend and I discovered the biggest flaw in the argument—it confuses looking for being thirsty or desperate. We all know the difference. Thirst and desperation never yield positive results. So yes, you should not be so consumed with your search for love that you become thirsty or desperate. If you're not sure if you've reached that point just ask a good friend.

We felt better at the end of our discussion as it was something we both were rattling with in our spirits. I encouraged her to keep working on self, to keep believing, to never be thirsty, and, most importantly, to keep looking for the love she's imagined. If a relationship is your goal, then by all means don't stop looking.

■ ■ ■

SPEND MY LIFE—MARRIAGE

*"Can I just see you every morning
when I open my eyes?"*

—*Posey, Benet & Nash*

*"It is not a lack of love, but a lack of
friendship that makes unhappy marriages."*

—*Friedrich Nietzsche*

ALWAYS A MAYBE, NEVER A YES

A couple of years ago, I had a sister-friend come to me distressed because as she saw it her husband had been taking her for granted. She told me the story and the basis for her distress, and she was right he was taking her for granted. They'd been married for over five years and she had become a "yes" and it was time for her to go back to being a "maybe." Basically, she was always available, always there, and always at his beckon call no matter what he did or did not do. And that needed to change.

Every Sunday and Monday men arm themselves with pizza, beer, chips, and so on to crowd around televisions across the country to watch whatever sport in season. I have a standing Sunday date with my boys every fall/winter/spring. We start off with football season, which then flows into basketball season. You pick your favorite teams, make your predictions, and argue about it all. A joyous cheer or a desperate sigh accompanies every great play and every missed opportunity. The point is men love competition even when they're not actually competing.

Although I knew the answer, I asked my sister-friend if she felt her husband had always taken her for granted. Of course not. He wouldn't be her husband if he had. But she was not quite sure what had changed or why it had changed. "You stopped being a maybe and became a yes," I said. She gave me that classic "what you talkin' 'bout Willis" look.

I remember when they first started dating and the way she acted then. She certainly didn't make getting her attention or her time easy for him. She was the prize and he had to prove his worthiness. I even remember her telling him just that…when they were dating. After getting married to him she slipped into the traditional role of wife. His meals prepared. His laundry done. His every whim and fancy were attended to by her. I am not knocking this because I do believe most women don't mind taking care of their husbands and their families even when they have careers outside the home. But she'd forgotten her power and the things that hooked him in the first place. It wasn't her cooking and cleaning skills—it was the prize.

She initially disagreed with me noting that she was not about to start playing games with her husband. Why not? Don't get me wrong; I am not talking about silly things that are contrived and upsetting. But what is wrong with a little cat and mouse to keep him interested and on his toes? Make him work for it sometimes. Her husband had begun to take her for granted because he could. She was so dependable and always available when he needed her—no matter what. It was up to her to make sure her husband knew that sometimes she was a maybe and he had to do some work to make her a yes.

So, I told her to go out with her girls (she couldn't recall the last time she had). Ask him to plan dinner at home once or twice a week. Establish a date night every week where he's responsible for the date. I encouraged her to remind him of the things that he used to do when he was trying to win her over. She needed to introduce the competition back into her relationship. And add a little sexual innuendo in all of this wouldn't hurt either. Don't make demands. Make requests that lead to rewards.

Let me tell you, she took my advice and it worked. She stopped sitting around waiting for him and started enjoying life beyond her career and marriage. She remained a good and faithful wife, but the moment she started living for herself again he responded. Two years later, they're still going strong and are happy. I'm not saying he's never taken her for granted since, but according to her and that bright smile it doesn't happen often.

My sister-friend's husband knows she is a maybe that he has to work for even though in the back of her mind she will always be a yes. Some things are best kept to ourselves.

■ ■ ■

YOU GET WHAT YOU ASK FOR

When I was growing up I was certain that my mother had psychic powers. Every time I would do something I shouldn't have done she'd know about it. Whether it was sneaking an extra piece of cake or staying up past my bedtime to watch TV this lady would always swoop in with her super powers and catch me.

Clearly, my mother was not and is not psychic, but she does possess a super power—women's intuition. When she became a mother, it evolved into a mother's intuition. Over the years, I have seen my sister-friends apply their super power in the craziest situations. They've known when their guy was: cheating; about to propose; and, unfortunately, was preparing to break it off. Women are psychic! Men, however, are not.

One of my sister-friends who has been married for over decade came to me this past Christmas season distraught.

Her husband had not bought her a gift for Christmas, her birthday, or anniversary for the past two years and she was upset. It seemed very strange to me coming from him because he is one of the most generous and thoughtful men I know. In fact, he'd consistently been way too generous to me and I know he loved his wife very much. Something else was up with this one.

He used to buy her gifts and the evidence was the bling on her body. What happened? She explained that two years ago he had mentioned that things were tight with business. It was the height of the recession and everyone was feeling the heat. My sister-friend being the team player she is told him not to worry about getting her a gift for Christmas or her birthday. Instead, she told him to focus on their daughter while he tried to get the business back in the black.

I applauded her! My sister-friend is a stay-at-home mother, but she has her own small business as well. But her husband has never even considered the money she's made from her business as a part of their family pot. It's her money. Therefore, her telling him not to worry about any lavish gifts was a great contribution. But what she'd failed to do is tell him that since they were now doing well she wanted the gifts to resume. She replied, "he should know that already we're doing great now." I had to use one of my auntie Gayle's phrases, "baby bye!"

I went on to explain that women often expect men to have the same super power they possess. It couldn't be further from the truth. Men are very cut and dry. We follow directions well, but often find it difficult to think beyond what is black and white. I'm not saying that brothers are stupid. We're just socialized differently and it is my belief that some of it is attributable to nature.

Too many of my sister-friends and other women get upset with men because they can't read their minds. In this case my sister-friend's husband had just been following what she'd told him and had not even thought beyond it. He wasn't being negligent. He just didn't know (or think).

The solution to the problem was simple: ask him to start giving gifts again. Tell him that you were being a team player when things were rough, but now that things are good you expect to receive gifts on those special days in your life. She did. And guess what he said? "OK, I didn't realize. I thought we were just going to focus on [their daughter]. No problem." And just like that she received a little red box (Cartier) for Christmas with the most gorgeous earrings I've seen.

I imagine she'll get something else spectacular for her birthday, anniversary, and other special occasions. All she had to do was ask and not assume her husband was a clairvoyant. Many of the disagreements that my sister-friends have with their guys are because they assume that men have the same super power. If you want something from your man or for him to do something try asking for it. He might have no idea that you want it.

■ ■ ■

(NOT SO) SUBTLE SUGGESTIONS

"You gotta pay the cost to be the boss." I can still hear my mother's voice telling me that as I was growing up in Chicago. It was her way of letting me know why she had the authority to tell me what to do.

Now I do pay the cost and I hate for people to tell me what to do. I think most of us do. But that sure doesn't stop us from telling other people what to do especially our significant others. I'm definitely a guilty one, but I know I need to change.

My sister-friend has been married for about seven years to a great guy. Her husband is gentle, fun, and so supportive of her and their son. They are the couple you want to be around because you feel the love. They joke with each other, are playfully difficult, and don't take themselves too seriously. It works!

It just so happens that my sister-friend's husband is famous, but you would never know it when you're around them. They epitomize the unaffected celebrity/wealthy couple by remaining real and down-to-earth. You're not going to catch them at the latest or hottest anything unless it's something they truly love. Their goal is not to impress anyone, but to be happy. Quite the change from many of the rich and famous people I know.

With all fame comes groupies and people who want to be around you purely because of your fame. In this instance, my sister-friend's husband has one friend who she believes is a fraud and is only friends with her husband because of his status. The guy takes liberties that even I don't take and I'm one of her best friends.

My sister-friend came to me a couple of months ago enraged. It turns out that her husband's friend had accompanied him across the world to Thailand. When they arrived his credit card didn't work and he called on her husband for help. Please note they were booked in a five-star hotel on the other side of the world. Her husband being the generous person he is picked up the bill.

It wasn't the money that upset my sister-friend because they have it like that. It was the principle. She was fed up with this guy using her husband and essentially her family. And she was preparing to give him a big 'ole piece of her mind. I might add that my sister-friend is no wallflower. It was going to be a showdown.

I cautioned her that although she may accomplish her goals with the guy she should strongly consider how her husband would react. In essence, she was planning on telling her husband he couldn't be friends with this guy anymore. Not only was this going to emasculate him, but also no grown man likes to be told what to do. Specifically, he doesn't want his wife choosing his friends especially when he doesn't do the same to her.

She was mad, but she took my advice and didn't say anything. I then told her to start making some (not so) subtle suggestions. As the guy did more to prove that he was a freeloader she should "suggest" certain ways for her husband to look at the situation. That way he could begin to see things as she had all along and form his own conclusions.

To my surprise and delight, my sister-friend took it a step further. She decided to start "suggesting" new friends to him. Last month I was at their house visiting and this very nice couple was there as well. I noticed how her husband had hit it off with them, particularly the man. Come to find out, my sister-friend had orchestrated this encounter so that her husband could see what kind of people he should be hanging around. Genius!

Just as I suspected, since the Thailand incident the guy has continued to overstep his boundaries. My sister-friend's husband hasn't completely cut him off, however, I think the end is in sight. The good news is that she is allowing him to come to the conclusion on his own without creating an issue between she and her husband in the process.

I think a lot of conflict in relationships could be avoided if one or both partners remember that they are partners not each other's parents. No grown person likes to be told what to do under any circumstance. And just because someone isn't vocal about their distaste for being bossed around doesn't mean it isn't having a negative effect on them and the relationship. The better alternative is to get creative and figure out a way to make some (not so) subtle suggestions.

■ ■ ■

FROM MY SISTER-FRIEND, MS. COPPER CUNNINGHAM

If someone offered me a large sum of money for the exact time I met Nathan Hale Williams I could not get it. I would have to leave that money where it is. How long have we been friends? Not sure. Seven years. Eight years. I am not sure. I am not sure because Nathan feels like part of my New York family for the best part of forever!

I met Nathan at one of my favorite New York spots, Native! *I considered Native my personal parlor. We had a Native family that was warm, wonderful, and supportive. Other attributes of many members of our Native family were brilliance, talent, commitment, philanthropic purpose, and a spiritual heart full of gratitude. Nathan embodies all of those attributes.*

True friendship is forged through years of commitment, respect, and shared values. Friends: show up, comfort, prop up, and encourage! *True friendship is peaceful, loving, supportive, and* no drama! *My conversations with Nathan have always been about what can make each of us better, and more fulfilled. How we can hear our better angels and fulfill the purposes for which we are called, I treasure that. I know when I talk to him I will get honesty and not duplicity.*

My funniest story is when a few of my dearest friends, including Nathan, had volunteered to help at a charity event. Nathan had invited one of his dearest friends, Dorian. Well it was a very, very hot day, we wanted to contribute to helping with the event, but we were not prepared to feel like we were slaves working on a plantation. Sweat was pouring off of all of us. When dehydration and dizziness set in, I knew I was done. I, with a couple of my confederates, looked at Nathan and Dorian, and we all said we were done! *We ended it for all of us, our suffering. We all ran off to* freedom! *We laugh about this now, but we weren't laughing then.*

I treasure my friendship with Nathan because he inspires me with his mind, heart, and soul. His mother, also my Soror [Delta Sigma Theta], is amazing! Wherever Nathan goes, I will only be a phone call away. He is a dear friend that I have grown to treasure.

About Ms. Copper Cunningham—The first part of my New York life consisted of a very successful and lucrative career in the creative realms of: acting, modeling, playwriting, and photojournalism. I studied photojournalism at The Columbia University Graduate School of Journalism. Acting: TV commercials, voiceovers, films, and soap operas. Modeling: national campaigns for Wendy's, Burger King, Seagram's, cover of Essence and Savvy Magazines, etc. Photojournalist: represented by Retna, an international agency for over fifteen years. After living many of my creative dreams, I wanted to give back to our community, so I became a special education educator, teaching severely emotionally disturbed and autistic children and young adults. I retired earlier this year, but will always cherish my years as a teacher as the most impact I have ever made. I taught these children with my whole heart.

DON'T SLEEP ON IT

We've all heard it before: Don't go to bed mad. It seems so simple, but so many of us don't practice this in our intimate relationships or with our families and friends. It's unfortunate because I believe this to be one of the tried and true adages that is paramount to maintaining healthy relationships.

A few months ago, I was shopping with my sister-friend who'd been recently married, for the third time. She is a very opinionated woman, yet with a lovable spirit. She is a walking contradiction because on someone else her opinionated nature would come off coarse and unlikable. For some reason, however, there is something about her that keeps her from being overbearing.

With that said, I can imagine that living with my sister-friend and her million plus opinions could prove to be difficult. It's probably why she's been married three times. While we were shopping (one of my least favorite pastimes) she recounted a recent argument that she had with her husband. In fact, the argument had extended over several days.

As she told me how wrong he was and how she'd made him suffer over the course of the argument I couldn't help to cringe. I didn't understand how she could get any pleasure from being in an extended argument with someone she loved and from "making him suffer." Personally, I'm a wreck when I'm in discord with anyone I love and care about. It wears me out.

Then, after about 30 minutes of this, I had enough. I also felt comfortable inserting my opinion into the conversation because she would do the same. "I don't think it's a good idea for you to let an argument linger that long," I asserted. "You probably did more damage to your relationship than you realize by not just nipping it in the bud the night you had the argument in the first place. 'Making him suffer' inflicts pain that might not be forgotten," I said perched high atop of my soapbox.

I went on to explain that with each argument that you have with someone that isn't resolved it has the potential to chip away at the foundation of your relationship. Naturally, all relationships will go through a moment of disagreement, and, at times, full-on argument. However, if we deal with it in the moment and don't let things fester they have less chance of becoming a cancer in your relationship.

"There's no way we could have resolved it then because he wasn't hearing me and it was late," she said in defense of her actions.

"I'm sure there was a way, you just didn't want to resolve it then. You said it yourself, you wanted to make him suffer," I admonished.

The reason why that adage about not going to bed mad is so true is because if that's the goal in your relationships, then you are forced to hash it out until you come to a resolution or you're at least back to center. It puts a burden on both parties to hear each other and move toward not letting negative feelings take residence in your spirit. You can only go to bed mad so many times before it starts chipping away at that foundation.

I then told her about a recent argument I had with a family member. It was so volatile that we both had to retreat to opposite ends of the house. We needed to cool off before we could hear each other. But once I did cool off, I prayed that I would approach the situation from a place of love and that we could resolve it to move forward. I went in to apologize for my behavior and to talk about the real basis for the argument. Thankfully, we were able to see the other person's perspective and went to sleep happy.

We think that our arguments are isolated incidents when in fact they culminate into the language of our relationships. "So, it depends on what you want your relationship to stand for and say," I said to my sister-friend who was actually listening for a change.

I could see she was beginning to have a breakthrough and joked, "Where were you when I got married the first time?" We both laughed and she agreed that she would try my approach the next time.

Like anything else in life relationships are a journey. We must take care of the relationship at all points on the journey, especially when it involves disagreements. Going to bed mad at a loved one only grows the bumps along the road. And the bigger the bump, the more potential for damage. So, if you're in an argument with your spouse or loved one resolve it right then and definitely don't sleep on it.

■ ■ ■

MIND THE GAP

When riding the Tube in London there is a phrase you hear over and over again, "Mind the Gap." The recorded message is your reminder that there is a large space between the platform and the train. It cautions you to be aware of the gap between the two so that you don't fall and hurt yourself. The same is true when gaps begin to form in relationships you must mind the gap before it gets too big and hurts your relationship.

At the end of last year, I was speaking with one of my sister-friends who has been experiencing a difficult time in her marriage. She and her husband both travel extensively for work and lately their schedules have not matched. This period followed another rough period in which they'd had a major disagreement on parenting.

"Find a way to close the gap between you right now or else it will grow, possibly to an irreparable point," I said.

We often seek to avoid confrontation and pain becoming ambivalent to situations because it's easier. Ambivalence is a cancer to a relationship. By not addressing their issues and allowing the distance to grow she was cultivating a bigger problem that could ultimately result in them being completely disconnected.

Our conversation also made me think of when I was practicing law. I hated it. The more I said I hated it; the more I did hate it. It was a self-fulfilling prophecy. It wasn't until someone gave me the wise advice to stop affirming my hatred of the job that I was able to bear the final two years of practice.

I encouraged my sister-friend to find the time to speak with her husband about ways they could work on their marriage. Also, to find moments for them to reconnect. I found out that they hadn't been on a vacation alone since their son was born eight years ago. They needed the opportunity before the distance grew too wide.

Two inverse principles were at play here. As with my practice of the law, that which you give energy/attention to grows in your spirit. For me, it was the hatred of my job. For my sister-friend, it was the disconnection she was feeling from her husband. Conversely, in relationships problems you ignore can also grow.

Over Valentine's Day weekend, my sister-friend and her husband went on a five-day Caribbean vacation. Nothing like some sand and sun (and cocktails) to put the pep back in your step and in your relationship. My plan worked far better than I imagined. Yesterday, I found out that she's pregnant again. And they've managed to rekindle their once strong romance. As a matter of fact, they're headed on another couple's vacation in two weeks. It took a minimal amount of effort, but yielded major results.

Relationships go through many seasons. Day-to-day living takes its toll and it's difficult to maintain throughout rough times. But we must be aware when distance begins to grow or when we become discordant with our partners. In that moment, it is time to put forth a big effort to close the distance to be in accord, and by all means mind the gap.

■ ■ ■

FROM MY SISTER-FRIEND, TURIYA MINTER

I met Nathan 3 years ago in the spring of 2012 at local hangout in Harlem called, Native. My cousin introduced me to this beautiful being—a ray of sunshine with a magnetic personality. I don't recall our first conversation or how we hit it off, but we had an instant connection. We've shared so many laughs I can't pinpoint just one, never a sad or dull moment, always fun, easy, and light in his presence. Any moment with Nathan that involves the music of Whitney Houston or Beyoncé is priceless! If you allow his iPod playlist to take over a party he'll make sure that you, "Dance with Somebody" like you never have before, you'll cut a rug to Whitney, and break a sweat and *will have had a blast doing so.*

The best advice he's ever given me is to always put a positive foot forward first. To lead with positivity, and always find the silver lining because even in the most dismal situations there's always a flipside. He has a genuine compliment and feels good vibes for you, a big hug, and that dynamic smile. My spirit cannot be down in his presence. A great listener, he gives sound advice from a male's perspective, and it's always fitting for whatever one might be going through. What I love about Nathan is that while he has many, many close friends, and best friends, he doesn't take any of it for granted. His friends mean a lot to him and he's sincere about it. It's not a numbers game, but rather the quality of the people that he surrounds himself with in his life.

About Turiya Minter—A simple girl from Southern California soaking up as much of New York City as I can while embracing every step of this journey; and collecting new friends along the way.

CHEATING: A CONCEPT

"Cheating is promising something that is unnatural for you and then behaving naturally. It's not cheating if you make your partner aware of it beforehand. It's about the lie, not so much the act."

- La Rivers

The quote is actually from one of my dearest and wisest sister-friends, La Rivers. In fact, I call her my muse and she often serves as my spiritual guide. She speaks the truth and is always right about people and their motivations. I agree with her. I think cheating is more about dishonesty than it is about the actual act. I just don't think many of us are ready to be honest in our relationships.

La and I have always said that cheating is not an absolute deal breaker for us. Yes, it's wrong, but why is it wrong? The truth is that when you make a commitment/promise to be monogamous, and then break that promise therein lies the deceit and problem. For me (and presumably for La), I don't think monogamy is the most natural thing and understand how hard it can be to maintain it. I know that's controversial, but it's what I honestly believe.

One of my other sister-friends suspects that her husband is cheating on her...again. They've been married for over fifteen years and have three kids. Throughout their marriage, they've both "stepped out" at various times—some trysts were discovered and others were not. Somehow, they have always managed to get beyond it and save their marriage. They are both committed to their vow of, "Till death do us part!"

My sister-friend told me that she'd found a woman's number in her husband's pants pocket. Classic scenario. Under most circumstances, I would've told my sister-friend not to overreact. But with her husband's track record it was probably what she thought it was. She was furious. I asked a simple question: "Why?" Hadn't they been down this road all too many times before—whether it be his acts of indiscretion or hers.

Needless to say, she couldn't believe my reaction. I knew it was time for some tough love. I was exhausted from the cycle and so I know she had to be too. I'd been through each of these "revelations" over the past fifteen years and just been there for her as a friend. Now, I had to be a real friend and tell her the truth.

"I don't see why you and [her husband] keep up this game." I went on to explain that they were clearly living the lie of monogamy. Every time one of them would get caught they'd have it out, make up, and vow to be monogamous. Instead, I suggested they be honest with each other and maybe try developing an understanding about extramarital activity.

You would've thought I told her to sacrifice a goat. She basically cursed me out and said, "That might work for YOU, but that's not gonna work in this house." Well, my dear, that's actually what's happening in your house already. I get it though. Anything beyond the traditional concept of marriage can be hard for many to digest.

I actually have several sister-friends who are married and have developed "understandings" with their husbands. Cheating is never an issue in any of those relationships. They fight about money and who's going to take the kids to school, but none of them have ever called me about their husband cheating.

Don't get me wrong; this is not a PSA for open marriages. The great majority of my sister-friends are in monogamous marriages and relationships (or at least I think they are). What I am saying is that the best relationships are built on honesty and trust. And the core crimes in cheating are dishonesty and a break of trust. Cheating involves sneaking around, covering up, and lying; it's a covert operation of dishonesty.

My suggestion to my sister-friend was that she and her husband talk openly and honestly about their true feelings.

For them, cheating was obviously not a deal breaker, but the endless cycle that they'd been in for years couldn't be healthy long-term. Maybe there was some way they could be honest and still live in their marriage.

I'm not sure if my sister-friend is going to take my advice. Often times the status quo, no matter how nonsensical, is much more comfortable than change. I am happy that our friendship survived our discussion. I took a risk, but I think I started her thinking about it differently. I know this for sure, if he or she does get caught cheating again she probably won't be calling me.

■ ■ ■

THE DANGERS OF AN AFFAIR

Smash (canceled) is one of my favorite new television shows for a number of reasons. I love its realistic in your face portrayal of the cutthroat entertainment business. The various storylines are focused on the production of a Broadway show based on the love life of Marilyn Monroe. Yet, it's not only Monroe's "sexcapades" that are front and center one of the lead characters (played by Debra Messing) is having a dangerous affair with one of the production's stars. The affair ends when the son of Messing's character devastatingly finds out.

Similarly, one of my sister-friends had been involved in a three-month affair with her personal trainer. My sister-friend has been married for about five years and has no kids. Her husband is not the nicest guy in the world and is far more devoted to his work than anything else, especially my sister-friend. In fact, her husband travels to South America for nearly two weeks out of each month.

I discovered the affair when I noticed a change in my sister-friend's behavior. She went from always being a bit sullen to all smiles, which was an indicator that some unmet needs were being met. I asked her point blank whether she was having an affair or not; and she reluctantly told me about the trainer. Naturally, what had started as casual flirting soon turned into much more. Without judgment, I warned her to be careful because these things never turn out good.

Over time, my sister-friend began to spend more time with the trainer. Overnight stays, dinner dates, and so on. The physical fling was quickly becoming emotional stirring up a recipe for disaster. Don't get me wrong, I don't condone an affair of any kind, but an affair of the heart is far more potentially explosive than a physical "jump off" from time-to-time.

Unfortunately, my fears became reality when my sister-friend and the trainer both caught serious feelings for each other. It's so easy to do when you're comparing a fantasy world to the real world of life and marriage. Real life can never compete with the passions of a secret rendezvous. Moreover, it's much easier to feel the romance when you're not looking at dirty socks, listening to snoring, or dealing with meddlesome mothers-in-law. All of these are perils of marriage and long-term relationships that come with being with someone day-to-day.

Surely, I understood my sister-friend had needs that weren't being met in her marriage. I reminded her that she needed to work that out *in* her marriage before venturing outside of it. By initiating and continuing this affair, she was undermining her relationship with her husband possibly to irreparable damage.

It's hard to tell someone on a roller coaster ride they're enjoying to get off; and so, she didn't take my advice. Fast-forward to a couple of weeks ago when all hell broke loose. Her husband found some undeleted text messages in her phone. He called the trainer who ultimately spilled the beans while professing his love for my sister-friend. As you can imagine, it sent their lives into a whirlwind.

The saddest part is that once confronted with the idea of being without her husband my sister-friend woke up. She realized she'd stupidly allowed herself to believe the hype and forget what was most important to her. She is trying to repair the damage she's caused and I hope it's not too late. Needless to say, she switched gyms and now works out with her girls.

Being faithful becomes increasingly more difficult when you're experiencing problems in your relationship. But you can't fix the problems by creating another one and starting an affair. Instead, focus on solving your issues in your current relationship and avoid the dangers of an affair.

■ ■ ■

FROM MY SISTER-FRIEND, TERRA WINSTON

You never forget the first time you meet Nathan. He bursts into your life like a swirling blur of fashion, fabulousness, and dimples. His star power is so bright that he easily eclipses the strongest personalities in any room. His magnetism draws you in and graciousness keeps you hooked on his every word. A decade ago I found myself sitting in a quiet corner at a friend's birthday party, utterly charmed by this lawyer/model/producer/director/author. That evening I became a fan.

However, I soon learned that there was so much more to him. One day while sipping tea at the kitchen table I stumbled upon the realization that he's a bona fide smarty-pants—an academic achiever of the highest caliber. A fierce game of Bid Whist taught me about Nathan's commitment to family (and his competitive streak). And during a long comforting conversation on his bestie's couch I realized how big his heart is. That was the night that I started calling him my friend.

Nathan's heart is what earns him the title of "The Girl's Best Friend." He can see each woman as she <u>really</u> is: flawed yet deserving of a flawless life. When doubts eat away at my confidence he reminds me of my worth. He refocuses my vision when I start thinking too small. He celebrates my beauty even on days when I don't always see it. Yet, he never avoids delivering the hard truths when a kick in the butt is the only way to get my attention. Nathan doesn't just give advice; he helps us overcome our challenges so that we can live our best lives. If that isn't a best friend—I don't know what is!

Let me leave you with a powerful lesson inspired by Nathan. His beautiful goddaughter, Jayden, was learning to play the viola. Like most seven-year-old children, Jayden had more enthusiasm than technique, and was required to practice several nights each week. One evening, while preparing for a recital, her mother noticed that she would leave the room before starting to play her piece. When asked about this odd behavior, she explained that Uncle

Nathan had told her that all performers should make an entrance. *The rest of the evening Jayden practiced her opening smile as much as her finger positioning, and went to bed satisfied with a job well done. Take note, my sisters. Don't shy away from the spotlight because you fear that you aren't good enough. Hold your head up high, put on your biggest smile, and step confidently on to center stage. Isn't it time that you made your* entrance?

About Terra Winston—Terra Winston, Ringleader of inTerractions (www.interractions.com), has had the privilege of helping thousands of people achieve what matters most through her coaching and leadership programs. A life-long learner, she has channeled her passions into success in multiple arenas, from engineering to human resources, from Corporate America to entrepreneurship.

YOU'VE GROWN, HE HASN'T

"You done changed," is a consistent joke between friends especially when one has achieved a certain level of success. It's particularly a joke for someone who has enjoyed or reached a certain level of celebrity. Jokes aside, people do change and grow regardless of success or fame. However, it can be a difficult road to travel in a relationship when one person has grown and the other person has not.

One of my sister-friends has been dating her husband since they were in high school in the inner city of St. Louis. For all intents and purposes, he's a great guy. More importantly, he has been supportive of my sister-friend's education and career although he has consistently maintained blue-collar jobs as a bus driver and a postal worker. On the other hand, my sister-friend has worked her way through higher education earning a MBA and Ph.D.

My sister-friend and I were on the phone a couple of weeks ago and she was lamenting over the fact that she often felt embarrassed by her husband in settings with her colleagues. Somewhere along the way she'd left him behind socially and definitely educationally. Often, she found herself not inviting him to events so she could avoid the bad feelings and the shame associated with those feelings.

She was asking for my advice, but even for me this was a tough one. I asked her whether she'd shared what she was learning with her husband like Nettie and Miss Celie in, *The Color Purple*. She had not.

The real problem then came out. She wasn't sure she wanted to educate him. She went on to confess that she'd grown so much, not just socially, but also in maturity that he no longer was attractive to her. They didn't like the same things anymore. Their discussions bored her. Ultimately, all of which made her not sexually attracted to him either. She'd seen the world and become the person she was intended to be. And that woman was different than the girl he'd met on the block when they were fourteen.

"It happens," I said plainly. It does happen, especially when people meet at such a young age and stay together. I believe it is why the divorce rate for people who marry after thirty is much lower than people who marry earlier. She certainly couldn't have known herself at fourteen or even when they got married at twenty-one.

My advice was to have a discussion with him about how she was feeling. Seek counseling and see if they could close the gap between them. Unfortunately, growing apart can be a lot more difficult than other marital issues that are merely circumstantial, like finances, and infidelity. I encouraged her to exhaust all that she could to save her marriage, but she ultimately had to do what would make her happy, and give her the freedom to live her best life.

Life is what it is and people grow apart. If you really do love and care for someone you owe it to each other to try to work it out. But it might be an unwinnable situation if you've grown and he has not.

(Update: They stayed together for two more years after I wrote this column. Her husband filed for a divorce citing the same reasons that she had. They were no longer the same people. He liked where he was and respected where she'd grown to be. The great news is they are amazing friends. She has remarried and he is in a long-term relationship).

■ ■ ■

FROM MY SISTER-FRIEND, DAPHNE DAVALIE

I am honored to say that I've known Nathan for over ten years. We met when I was Associate Fashion Editor at Trace Magazine, *an independent monthly highlighting transcultural talent on the rise. One afternoon, from my dorm room at Rutgers University, I opened an email from my Editor-In-Chief. I was pleasantly surprised to learn that he wanted me to judge aspiring fashion stylists for a chance to style actress/model Eva Marcille for a* Trace *cover story. The first production meeting was about a week later. When I arrived, Nathan greeted me with a warm smile and hello, and then for the first time in my life I heard someone call me "gorgeous".*

One Sunday, Nathan and I decided to reconnect over brunch at Agave NYC. On my way over, he let me know that he was bringing a guest to join us. Of course, I thought the more the merrier. It's important to note that a little before this we caught up over drinks and discussed a girlfriend's favorite topics: love, dating, & relationships. He shared some details about a certain gentleman he decided to drop partially because of his questionable fashion choices and some extra pounds. Clearly, his guest at brunch was way more handsome and definitely in great shape. A few mimosas too many, and I blurted out, "Well I'm glad you brought him and left that other big one alone, chile!" Needless to say, I wasn't exactly supposed to share that information and Nathan's eyes grew wide with shock. Luckily, his guest didn't seem too phased by it and we continued the brunch without me sticking my foot in my mouth.

Nathan is a living well of advice and wisdom, not in words, but in action.

My favorite Nathan quotes include:

(1) "If opportunity doesn't knock, build a door."
(2) "Gotta make sure your paperwork is in order, first."

Nathan is, and always has been, one of my greatest inspirations. In my personal life, he's like my Oprah. When I do finally meet Oprah I'm sure he'll be the first person I mention. He's definitely one of the most talented Black producers I know. At the same time, this multi-talented, award winning mega producer is also humble, spiritual, and all the way real. The brother can write, produce, act, distribute, direct and seal the deal with a Chi-town swag that reminds you why he's the ultimate Girl's Best Friend!! For sure, you can always count on Nathan for a fun and fabulous time whether it's a Tuesday networking mixer or Saturday night turn up. He's the only person I know who can craft an inspirational cuss combo that inspires you to do something great.

About Daphne Davalie—Daphne is a creative at heart with a head for business. Most recently, she co-produced her first short documentary film honoring prominent African-American alumni from Columbia Business School. The documentary is entitled, 100 Thank You's: A Tribute to African-American CBS Alumni. *She is a 2016 graduate of Columbia Business School. Prior to her foray into the business of entertainment, she built a career in fashion editorial and book publishing. Currently, she lives in Harlem, NY and works in entertainment finance in Stamford, CT.*

WHAT ARE WE ARGUING ABOUT?

I absolutely hate to argue! It is rare that I argue with my friends and I certainly try not to argue in my intimate relationships. But the lawyer in me loves a good debate. I do believe that adhering to some core principles of debate would alleviate a lot of arguments.

- Listen to your opponent's position.
- Don't speak until they're time is up.
- Only debate the points raised in their argument.

Over the holiday weekend I went to visit my best sister-friend and her husband to celebrate their son's fifth birthday. I absolutely love being around them because they renew my belief that the black family is intact and thriving. Moreover, they are both highly intelligent and entertaining. I know there are no perfect couples, but the way they run their marriage is a great standard to emulate and encourage.

After putting the kids to bed, we all gathered to watch the NFL Playoffs and chat. My sister-friend and her husband, who is a former pro athlete, are both Real *Housewives of Atlanta* fans. (Don't tell him I told you.) He said he'd heard that they'd made thirty thousand dollars per episode and we began to debate the accuracy of the information. I thought that was high for cable and he agreed with me. He then told my sister-friend, "See, I told you!"

They began a debate over whether or not they'd previously debated this topic and how he'd come upon the salary information. It was a hilarious, harmless squabble over something trivial, but it did go on for thirty minutes. In fact, my sister-friend's mom looked at her watch and said to me, "Let's see how long this goes." I finally interjected that the sole reason for the disagreement was because they were arguing two different points. When, in reality, they did not disagree with each other on either point.

The next night, my sister-friend's husband and I, got into a similar friendly mental joust over who was more authentic: Jay-Z or Kanye. I argued that they were equally authentic to who they are and their backgrounds. I asserted that what he really meant was that Kanye was more unique as a rapper because of the subject matter that he chose to rap about on his records. This debate went on even longer until we realized again that we actually agreed with each other rendering the disagreement moot.

Our debates were all in fun and full of mutual respect on all sides. But it got me to thinking about the origin of most arguments. It usually involves two people not listening to each other's point of view and arguing two different points. Think about the last argument you had. More than likely, you were not arguing about the same thing. All the while complaining that the other person wasn't hearing you.

My analysis of our weekend debates was that we were all so consumed about being right and proving the other person wrong we didn't take the moment to listen openly to their position. We cut each other off. Dismissed the other's points. And ultimately realized that we both had valid positions. Once we opened our ears, were courteous, and talked directly to the raised points there was no longer any issue.

I know it sounds simple. Because it is! The next time you're on the brink of an argument, pull yourself back and start listening. Remember those principles and avoid the never fruitful act of arguing altogether. If you are going to argue at least know what you're arguing about.

■ ■ ■

IS FOREVER TOO MUCH PRESSURE?

"Till death do us part." Marriage is rooted in the concept of a life-long commitment between two people that so many of us aspire to have. And although I firmly believe in the many benefits of marriage the concept of forever might be too much pressure, and thus detrimental to that very goal.

In the contemporary Western world, marriage is viewed as a legal and spiritual bond between two people. The history of marriage, however, tells a different story. Marriages were more business and less love in the not too far off past. It was about forming alliances between families, strengthening blood lines, and in many cases, adding to a family's workforce. The woman in the marriage was certainly not seen as an equal to her man.

Thankfully, things have progressed and times have changed. Women are no longer viewed as property in most societies and the goal of marriage is to formalize an eternal bond with the one you love. It is why many couples today choose to write their own vows based on their goals and views about the relationship they are entering. Consequently, we have adopted a far more romantic and emotional approach to marriage.

In many instances, the progress is a good thing. Yet, using love as the predominant basis for marriage can prove to be problematic. We all know that people change over time. The things you loved about a person five years ago might be the things that get on your last nerve today. Emotions, in general, are volatile so much so that betting that your feelings about someone will be the same forty years from now is a bad bet.

Now, don't get me wrong, I am not saying that forever is impossible or that it should not be a goal in marriage. I believe that it should be. However, the emphasis that we place on "making it work forever" or "staying together until we die" is so much pressure that we forget to live in and enjoy the moment. Our focus on the future deprives our present emotions and feelings of their validity.

I read a book by Eckhart Tolle titled, *The Power of Now*, which I think prescribes a healthier way to live and to approach any relationship, particularly marriage. Instead of focusing on some far-off goal; it is a better practice to live and love for today. By doing so you are focused on your partner as they are right now. Not how they were yesterday or how they will be when they are seventy-five. More importantly, it allows you to change together, and it allows your love for each other to change.

The presumption that you can predict forever is a false one we all know to be true. I have often seen my married friends get preoccupied in "trying to make it work" than truly living and appreciating each other in the now. I think more marriages and committed relationships would reach forever without the pressure of thinking about it.

■ ■ ■

WE ARE FAMILY— FAMILY & FRIENDS

"I got all my sisters with me."

—Nile Rodgers

"Cherish your human connections - your relationships with friends and family."

—Joseph Brodsky

WHAT ABOUT YOUR FRIENDS?

In 1992, the singing group, TLC had a song, "What About Your Friends?" I loved that song and the video (because of the new dance moves they introduced). Yet, it's not just a catchy 90's song. The lyrics to the chorus are poignant about friendships: "What about your friends, will they stand their ground...will they let you down...or will they turn their backs on you."

If you've lived long enough you've experienced disappointing friendships that you thought would last, but didn't. For various reasons, some friends come and go; that's just the way it is. I, however, strongly believe in the adage that people enter your life for a reason, a season, or a lifetime so I tend not to sweat it too long.

Unfortunately, I have found that the female friends I have lost over the years ultimately have something to do with a man. And I'm definitely not a chauvinist, but the male friends I've lost have almost never had anything to do with a woman. I believe it is how women are socialized to think they need a man in their life to be complete, and are willing to sacrifice friendships to get and keep one.

One of my sister-friends met the "man of her dreams" about a year ago. She's in her early forties and divorced with no children. She was married and divorced in her early twenties so her search for love has been an almost twenty-year journey. Gorgeous and smart she's never had any difficulty finding men to date, but it was always the same failing story.

I wouldn't call my sister-friend desperate, but there was a noticeable shift in her attitude between the ages of thirty-seven and forty. It was clear that she was much more aware of her mortality and that proverbial ticking clock. She still wanted children and having your first child at forty-something could be problematic. Time was not on her side and she knew it.

With that said, my sister-friend was not outwardly consumed by her thirst for a man and a family. She was always out with us taking vacations, nights on the town, and so on. She was definitely enjoying her life and her friends were a big part of that enjoyment. Many of us were single and we relied on each other to fill that lonely gap. And we are all great friends.

When she started dating her boyfriend we began to see less and less of her. It didn't bother me so much because I'm pretty consumed at the beginning of a relationship myself. It's that time when you're getting to know someone and with all of the other strains on a busy New York schedule it's difficult to fit everyone into it. Our other friends, on the other hand, had concerns from the beginning.

My other friends convinced me to participate in a "friend-tervention." They wanted to express how excited we were for her, but that we missed her and would like to see her at least some time. That didn't go so well, to say the least. In essence, she told us to mind our business and if we couldn't just be happy for her, then we weren't really her friends in the first place. Okay!!! We backed off.

Slowly, but surely she became more and more distant. It would be weeks and months that we would not hear from her. She then completely disconnected from all of us. Feeling hurt by this, I sent her an e-mail (since she was not returning my calls) telling her how much I cared about her and wanted the best for her. I also warned her that she could not disrespect her friendships like she had been. Not wishing ill will on her relationship, but if something were to happen with the relationship she would be looking to us to help her pick up the pieces. It's not so easy if you've alienated them all in the process. She never responded.

I ran into her last week at a function for an artist friend we have in common. All night I could tell she was avoiding me. I chased her down because I hadn't seen her in almost a year. She was clearly on edge as we went through the usual pleasantries. Finally, I asked her about her man and how they were doing. I had hit a sore spot. Sensing that she was uncomfortable I changed the subject and invited her to join me for a drink after the showing.

Thankfully, she agreed to join me for the drink. As we caught up, she opened up that the guy had been cheating on her since they first got together with multiple women. He'd even passed along an STD. She was heartbroken and embarrassed; pretty much flying solo for the last few months. She was ashamed of the way she had treated her friends and thought the damage she'd done was irreparable.

My sister-friend believed that she had no one to turn to for support. I assured her that, for me, my friendship was non-negotiable. Once I care about someone I will always care about him or her. Although I didn't agree with her motivations, I understood. You have to take people for who they are and where they are in their lives. The past was best left in the past and we were cool. I would be there for her.

It was a valuable lesson for many women (and men) who forsake their friendships for a romantic relationship. You need the love of a *partner and* the love of friends. And if your partner doesn't appreciate and understand that you need to maintain friendships you might want to reexamine your relationship. If you're in a relationship and feeling like you've lost contact with your friends, remember just ask yourself, "What about [my] friends?"

■ ■ ■

RECONNECT WITH OLD FRIENDS

Storms don't only bring clouds. A storm can bring positive opportunities if you seek something good from it. Last week, New York City was hit by a snow storm in the middle of October. Many looked at it as a hindrance to their Saturday plans. For me, and one of my best sister-friends, it was a chance to reconnect and catch up. It was something that I didn't realize I needed until we did it.

It's no secret that I love my friends. I have been very blessed to encounter and be surrounded by some of the best people I think the world has to offer. I also pat myself on the back because I must be a good friend as I have been friends with most of them for twenty to forty-one years. You can't be too bad with that sort of friendship track record.

Although most of my friends and I have long-standing friendships I also have met some great new people in my life. Ironically, I tend to spend more time with the new people than I do with the old friends. It's certainly not by conscious choice, but I do think there is a familiarity that comes with a twenty-year friendship that doesn't crave or require the constant interaction. No matter how long the time between visits you always pick up where you left off.

As I have said, I was downtown when the storm started nearby one of my best sister-friend's apartments who I've known for forty plus years. It had been a minute since we'd seen each other so I sent a text to see if she and her husband were home. They responded, "Yes! Come over!" Thankfully, I was merely minutes away and didn't have to deal with the weather too much.

Once I was there, it was as it always is—like home. I kicked off my shoes, poured a glass of wine, and saddled up on the sofa. This was familiar because the last time we spent a day like this was unfortunately after 9/11. But this occasion was nothing, but joyous because as much as I love my sister-friend, I love her husband a lot too. They both are super intelligent and super fun and I get super inspired when I am around them.

We then got to talking about how much my sister-friend and I don't see each other on a regular basis. She's always out with her "new" friends and I'm always out with mine. True, we have a bond that transcends mere clubbing and dinners. However, we started discussing why we had taken it for granted. Especially since our bond is so special and spirit-feeding to the both of us.

Quite frankly, we couldn't come up with a reason why our in-person interactions were few and far between other than we were taking our friendship's durability for granted. It wasn't just about face time it was about the nurturing we get from each other when we're close. There is no perspective like a friend who has known you and your family your entire life.

By the end of my day with my sister-friend and her husband, I felt rejuvenated and inspired to go back into the world and conquer the life storms that we all face. We had turned what could've been a bad day into something that was positive and uplifting. We had relationship therapy, job therapy, friendship therapy, and life therapy. We worked on each other's spirits in a way you can only do with someone who has known you that long.

It taught me that I need to make a concerted effort to connect with my old friends more. There's a reason why they've withstood the test of time when so many other people have come in and out of my life. Old friends, the good ones, get you to your core and nourish your soul in the same way an old pair of sweats makes you feel on a lazy Sunday afternoon.

As you go about your business, I hope to continually remind you to take care of you. We give so much to others that we forget those simple things that feed and refresh our spirits. Maybe it's time that you give yourself a boost by reconnecting with some dear old friends.

■ ■ ■

FROM MY SISTER-FRIEND, QIANA HAIR-BROWN

Nathan and I met through a mutual friend in 2010. Nathan was one of the hottest club promoters in New York City I frequently attended. I'd been going through a rough time trying to get into the film business and wanting to learn how to produce movies. I had no idea Nathan was the perfect person to look to for guidance. To the world, Nathan is a celebrity. To me, he is my friend. It wasn't until I became his assistant, when I learned who I was actually working with - Nathan Hale Williams - Producer of Dirty Laundry, The Ski Trip *and star of reality show,* Girls Who Like Boys Who Like Boys. *I immediately became nervous and scared.*

I've always placed Nathan on a high pedal stool. Always. He's smart, funny, intelligent, and he is loyal. Let's not leave out he is highly educated. I never had the privilege of attending an Ivy League school, and I felt if I would represent Nathan, I should have a solid background. He quickly disregarded my feelings and continued to encourage me and helped me to understand that it's not the level of education you have, but your character that matters most. You *can be whatever you want to be. You have only to keep going, keep pushing, and never give up. My confidence instantly raised. Nathan's words to me: Tell your own story. You'll never know who you will inspire.*

The Girl's Best Friend is Nathan Hale Williams. He's an ear when you need someone to listen, he is a voice when you need your spirit uplifted, and he is a shoulder when you need to cleanse your soul. He may not always tell you what you want to hear, but he will tell you what you need to hear. Nathan has the most powerful voice ever heard. I am amazed at how much his spirit is intertwined with others. Near or far, Nathan can feel when you are in need of a little motivation. He has left me speechless often.

About Qiana Hair-Brown—Qiana is a producer, writer, and lover of fine art. Mrs. Brown is a mother of two beautiful children, a wife, and is a lover of life. Her favorite quote is: "Giving up is not an option - it never is."

THANKSGIVING: A CELEBRATION OF FRIENDS

For the first time in the nineteen years since I left Chicago, I'm unable to go home due to a hectic work schedule. Needless to say, I was bummed about breaking my long-standing tradition, but grateful to be working in these difficult times. For me, it's not just about family and eating; Thanksgiving is the time I catch up with my friends. Thankfully, my best friend Danielle is not going home to Chicago either and lives nearby in New Jersey so I will spend Thanksgiving with she and her family (considered my family too).

Each Thanksgiving, I'm especially grateful for the enduring friendships that I have established and enjoy. Yes, I love my family and usually spend the first part of the day with them. However, I really look forward to traveling to my other BFF Andrea's house where all of us get together to play cards, drink Sangria, laugh, and of course, eat some more. As an only child, my friends are truly the only brothers and sisters I have. And I cherish them more and more each year.

As you get older, people will come in and out of your life. Over the past two years, I have lost a handful of friends, which was something new for me. At first, it was very difficult and I took it really hard. As they say, time heals all wounds and I decided to focus on the great and long-lasting relationships that remain strong. Everyone isn't supposed to stay in your life forever, nor should they. But the ones that do should be celebrated every chance you get and what better time than during Thanksgiving and the holidays.

One thing I have learned to be true that in order to have good friends you have to be a good friend. In my definition, it is about mutual respect, admiration, and acceptance—all of which I've enjoyed for forty-one years with my friends. To think, that I've known my best friends that long is unbelievable and I'm grateful for their presence in my life. Constantly, I remind myself to let them know what they mean to me and to thank them for being a friend.

Sharing laughs and reminiscing about stories of the past is really my favorite part of the holiday season. It is the time we take a pause from our busy lives to enjoy the company of our loved ones. This Thanksgiving I'm challenging myself to do something I've never done before. I'm going to write all of my friends letters and let them know how much I love them. Not an e-mail, a text, or a

Facebook post, but an actual old-fashioned letter. We've long stopped exchanging gifts because the focus is on the kids, but I couldn't think of a better gift to give.

I challenge us all not to only remember our families this holiday season, but don't forget to take a moment out to celebrate your friends. I always sing this to my friends, "If you threw a party, invited everyone you knew, you would see the biggest gift would be from me, and the card attached would say, 'Thank you for Being a Friend." What ways will you celebrate your friends this holiday season?

■ ■ ■

COUNT ON ME

"Lots of people want to ride with you in the limo, but what you want is someone who will take the bus with you when the limo breaks down." – Oprah Winfrey.

Everyone who knows me knows that Oprah (along with Whitney & Beyoncé) is my best friend in my head. From the time I was a child in Chicago, I have learned so much from just watching and reading what she has had to say over the last thirty years. As I have enjoyed my own success over the years, the aforementioned quote has done me a world of good. The quickest way to tell who your real friends are is to need something—a favor or some help.

I truly believe that you do things for people because you want to and you set yourself up for disappointment if you expect anything in return. It is why when I do something for someone it is truly because I want to do it. With that said, I love helping people and I've committed myself to being a supportive person not only to my friends, but also my acquaintances. I even extend a helping hand to people I don't know when the request is appropriate, within my ability, and for the good. So many people have helped me that I have to pay it forward and do the same.

Working in the entertainment business can be a pretty tricky endeavor. You have so many "friends." When the going is great you have tons of them hanging around. However, if you ever find yourself in a rough patch or not at the top of your game the many become few. Perfect example is that one of my sister-friends who has helped so many people is planning a series of events. She reached out to some of her "fabulous" friends in entertainment to host the events and no one replied. Crickets!

Earlier this week, she called me so disappointed that none of these people who she had helped along the way were willing to do something so simple. "I wasn't calling asking to borrow money or dog sit for me for a week. I only asked them to add their names to an event for a good cause," she lamented. Unfortunately, none of them even had the decency to respond with a "no."

Along the same lines, another sister-friend who was once rich and a part of the New York elite crowd fell on hard times. She could no longer afford the thousand-dollar gala tickets or the summer house in the Hamptons. Just as quickly as her money disappeared so did her friends and "membership" in that society. Quickly, she found out who her real friends were. As I said to her, it was a blessing as now she is back on top, but with the knowledge of who is really in her corner. Wisdom is an invaluable commodity.

Unfortunately, the world is full of fake and phony people. It seems the number grows exponentially the more fame and/or money you get. Like the Notorious B.I.G. said, "Mo' Money, Mo' Problems." But all you have to do is need something yourself to determine whether or not you can count on your friends.

■ ■ ■

NO NEW FRIENDS

"I stay down with my day one [friends]," raps Drake in the DJ Khaled hit, 'No New Friends.' Certainly, I can relate to this sentiment as I have known my best friends for most of my life. It's one of the reasons I enjoy going home for Thanksgiving because it's the time we all get together. And it is also why after some difficult patches with less seasoned friendships, I was also singing, "No New Friends." But that's not a good thing.

Over the past couple of years, I have had friend drama that was suitable for any of those shows I hate to admit I watch. Misunderstandings, false accusations, and other bad behavior was flying back and forth from both sides. It shook me to my core because it was definitely not what I was used to inside the confines of a friendship. I have known two of my best friends, Andrea and Antonious, literally my entire life and two of my others, Danielle and

Dorian, for twenty-plus years. In all of that time, I have never had an argument with any of them.

It was about a month ago that I had resigned myself not to meet anyone new. (I was on the verge of making the same proclamation with regard to dating as well). I was just going to stick with what I knew and that was it. Not only is that unrealistic it is also unhealthy for your spirit.

Closing myself off was a protective measure that was rooted in the fear of getting my feelings hurt again. But doing anything out of fear is always going to yield a bad result, particularly for someone like me who loves people and meeting new people. It didn't feel right to be that intentional about something negative.

Then, just as the universe does, a co-worker and I decided to go out to lunch. At first, I was determined to keep it on the "hello" and "goodbye" level. I wasn't going to share anything about myself, except the surface stuff. It would be nice to have a lunch buddy, but I was not looking for any new friends. We had a ball at lunch and clicked on so many levels. But no new friends, I said!

Thankfully, my co-worker didn't know of my recently implemented rule and we kept talking. I decided that I would open up my spirit and be receptive to whatever developed. It has been amazing to have someone to speak to in the office and a very enjoyable friendship seems to be forming. Had I remained closed that wouldn't have happened and it has been a blessing.

People may hurt us along the way and a natural reaction is to put up our defenses and shut out the rest of the world. We are truly here for each other. You can't fully live your life without being open to new experiences, new things, and new people. You might just miss a major blessing if you resolve to say, "No new friends."

(Update: The work friend referenced became one of my dearest friends, Shauna Kamiel whose essay preceded this in the book. I am so grateful I didn't stay in the negative place and opened my spirit. She is no longer a new friend.)

■ ■ ■

GOOD FRIENDS MAKE GREAT HUSBANDS

The male/female friendship can be a difficult one because often times dating and sexual attraction can get in the way. The basis of all friendships is some sort of attraction and if it's with the opposite sex problems can arise. I do think it can also be a good thing if both the man and the woman are on the same page.

Recently, a sister-friend discovered that a guy she'd known for a couple of years, as a friend, was attracted to her. It was a surprise to her because they'd always had a platonic and fun friendship. At first, she was apprehensive about dating him, but when he wouldn't relent she gave in and they went out. What she discovered was that in the forum of a date she was even more attracted to him than she'd previously thought.

This particular sister-friend has been known to be a player so she continued to date other guys while dating her "friend." Slowly, but surely the other guys disappeared and there was just this guy who had not quite moved into boyfriend realm. She can be very guarded and tends to take moving to the official step very slowly. Months went by and I kept hearing this guy's name. I knew something more serious was going on even if she wasn't in the position to admit it.

I was on social media and she'd changed her relationship status. It shocked me and made me very happy at the same time. For someone so fiercely private, it was a surprise that she would broadcast anything personal like that in such a public forum. We don't do that. Yet, I was even happier she was at a point where it meant enough to her to step outside of her comfort zone.

I loved the guy with which she was now, "in a relationship." He was friendly, smart, and clearly concerned about her needs. He also struck me as someone who liked my sister-friend 'as is' and had no desire to change who she is. Because their relationship was built on a foundation of friendship they both knew exactly what they were getting and liked it.

It made me consider all of the successful relationships that I know. They are all rooted in a great friendship. When my best friend got married, it was difficult for me to accept that I was no longer her true 'best friend,' but that is the way it should be. It is clear that she and her husband are each other's best friends. And I am sure when things get rough (as they do for everyone) it is their friendship that makes it easier.

Personally, I can say the same thing. My long-term relationship lasted as long as it did because we were friends first before we got romantic. If the statistics add up correctly it looks like my sister-friend who is now involved with her friend has a great chance for success in the relationship—maybe even marriage.

If you're looking for the guy for you maybe you don't have to look too far—he might already be a friend. Naturally, the feeling has to be mutual, but romantic relationships rooted in great friendships seem to be stronger than ones that are not. Don't count out your good friend he might make a great husband.

(Update: I was onto something and so was my sister-friend. They are the disgustingly happy couple that you want to hate, but you just can't. They are wonderful together as husband and wife. And, of course, best friends.)

■ ■ ■

FROM MY SISTER-FRIEND, DANIELLE MOODIE-MILLS

I've known the fabulous Mr. Williams for over a decade. We met when he was filming the reality TV show, The American Candidate, and then again, a year later in Washington, D.C. through a mutual friend. The final time we met, and he actually remembered me…LOL, was at a GLAAD media awards in LA in the early 2000s.

When we met the third time and I teased him for not remembering me, he joked, looked me up and down and said, "Well, I will never forget this fierceness ever again." He showered me with flattery—who could be mad after that?

Since then, my wife and I have come to Nathan for advice and support regarding the entertainment business. We were considering doing a reality TV show, but he was adamantly against it. He told me how much he loved my wife and I and admired our marriage and didn't want to see it meet the reality TV curse. He said, "How many happily married couples exist after reality TV?" We never did the show and have been happily married going on eight years now.

Nathan is The Girl's Best Friend, because he is the honest, loving, and real big brother every girl needs. He will tell you when you are cute and when your attitude must be fixed for you to get what you want and deserve. He's a doll and anyone lucky enough to enter into his orbit will never stop smiling or shining from the glow that emanates from him.

About Danielle Moodie-Mills—Danielle is the host of #WokeAF on SiriusXM Progress channel 127. She is also a Vice President of Public Affairs at SKDKnickerbocker, a public affairs, PR and crisis communication firm. Danielle has spent her career speaking truth to power and advocating for LGBTQ equality and social justice.

WATCH THE COMPANY HE KEEPS

Birds of a feather flock together! A truer statement couldn't be said. A person's friends are a clear indication of who they are. It is why when dating someone you should definitely watch the company he keeps.

A month ago, my sister-friend and I were talking about a guy she'd been dating for close to three months. She was so excited about him and they'd had a great time. Her friends had met him, but she hadn't met his friends. I encouraged meeting his friends as soon as possible.

"I get that you don't want to bring your friends around in the early stages, but at three months you should know at least one or two of his friends," I said. She chalked it up to them being so wrapped up in each other and not really having the opportunity. I bought it, but I'm always suspicious of someone who doesn't want you to meet their friends or doesn't have any.

It has been my experience that people who don't have at least one childhood friend around are usually crazy. My sister-friend took my advice and asked him to set up a time for her to meet his friends. And they did.

The night out went so "well" that my friend thought the she was being "Punk'd" and kept looking for Ashton Kutcher. One of his friends showed up to drinks already drunk and "lifted" from some other substance. The other friend, who is married, showed up with a date that wasn't his wife. And the somewhat normal friend didn't have any money to pay the bill at the end. Needless to say, it was a disaster and her boyfriend claimed that it was abnormal. She bought it. I didn't.

Fast forward to last week when we met for drinks. Unfortunately, my prediction was correct. The guy had turned out to be a far cry from the representative he'd sent the first ninety days of their relationship. In fact, he was much closer to his friends. He liked to drink a lot, get high, had been borrowing money to take her out, and hit on a couple of her friends. I mean, I'm good at calling things, but this one was too much. Truth is stranger than fiction.

I was sad for my sister-friend that it didn't work out for her. But, glad she'd gotten rid of the guy before she was too invested in him. As she discovered, a little Inspector Gadget into his friends and how they were proved to reveal a lot about him. Good ridden to bad rubbish.

The ninety-day representative rule is the truth. It usually takes ninety days to find out how much of the representative you're getting from someone. If you want to get a quicker indication of who he truly is watch the company he keeps.

■ ■ ■

MIND YOUR BUSINESS

"Keep your business out of the street!" Most of us have heard this while growing up and throughout our lives. My family, in particular, is a very private one. We generally keep what goes on within in our family inside the family. As I have gotten older, the wisdom of that practice has become more apparent, especially when it comes to dating and relationships.

Remember back in high school when we all first started dating we told all of our business. The minute we liked someone all of our friends knew and usually most of the school. It was our first "piece of business" and we couldn't wait to share it. Slowly, but surely, we discovered the pitfalls of having everyone in your business.

One of my sister-friends has been married for three years. We've known each other for almost twenty years and for the majority of that time she's always had a big mouth. She's a sweetheart, but you definitely want to watch what you say to her. For that reason, she's one of my sister-friends that I have to manage.

When she first got married she had a bunch of girlfriends that she'd met since we've been adults. These other ladies were not mutual friends and I just didn't trust them. But I would hang out with them when my sister-friend would invite me along. As I attended more and more outings, I realized that my sister-friend told an awful lot of she and her husband's personal business.

Big mouth and all, my sister-friend really has it together. Plus, her husband is one of those ideal "good men." He is very attractive, successful, caring, and thoughtful. The women she was hanging out with weren't on the same level. They were all single. I thought it was a recipe for disaster.

One day, I told my sister-friend that I thought she should be more protective of her family business. She was offended by my advice. I then recounted how I had heard her discuss many topics with these ladies that I felt were inappropriate. She'd discussed their arguments, their sex life, his family problems, and some financial issues he'd had from his past. Way too much!

She quickly and not so politely told me to mind *my* business. It was her business and her friends; she could do what she wanted to do. Amen, sister. Float on chicken bone. But I warned her, "Mark my words you will get burned!" From then on, I declined the invitations to hang out with her and that group of women.

About a year ago, my sister-friend invited me out for brunch. We hadn't seen each other in a minute so I was very excited. Well, before I could sit down good she was in tears. She was distraught because her husband had moved out. He had said it was temporary, but she was fearful that he might not come back.

Turns out, one of her "friends" was a human tape recorder. She made an advance on her husband and while doing so spilled everything that my sister-friend had shared with her. Imagine a man hearing *all* of his personal business parroted back to him by a woman whom he barely knew and the information source is his own wife. Thankfully, my sister-friend's husband is a stand-up guy and rebuked the woman's advances.

Even still, he felt betrayed by his wife and they'd already been having some difficulties. He moved out to evaluate their marriage and make some decisions. It was a hard lesson to learn, but a necessary one. I knew something like that was going to happen. It didn't seem right for her to share so much with people she didn't know that well.

My sister-friend and her husband went to counseling and she had one-on-one sessions as well. They were able to work it out and stay together. But imagine if she was married to a different man with a lot less integrity. She still has a big mouth, but not about her business. She'll tell yours, however, she's learned to keep her own business to herself.

I love the phrase, "not everyone deserves a front row seat to your life." It is the truth! I hear so many women sharing intimate details of their relationships with other people. It always makes me cringe. Now, your good girlfriend of thirty years is one thing because we all need a confidant and sounding board. Other than that, I suggest you mind your business and keep it out of the street.

■ ■ ■

FROM MY SISTER-FRIEND, TONI Y. LONG

I have known Nathan for over twelve years. I met Nathan when he and the director, Maurice Jamal were working on their film, Dirty Laundry. *I was with a film distribution company at the time and the project was pitched to us. I knew it was not for the company, but wanted to help. Nathan and Maurice came to Los Angeles to find talent and investors. We had dinner, and I offered my advice on the project. Bonding over being attorneys and our work in the industry we have been fast friends ever since.*

When we first met, I was shocked to meet Nathan. All of my email correspondence had been with Maurice. He introduced Nathan (who I knew from his role in the film, The Ski Trip*), and I noted, as is my way, what a bitch that character was! Nathan took the ribbing in stride, and we all had a great laugh about that character. I was delighted to discover he is nothing like the character, which is a testament to his acting talent because that character was a real piece of work.*

I cannot settle on one piece of advice. Nathan and I share a lot of advice back and forth. Because of the respect I have for him, when he speaks, I listen. His knowledge was on full display when we first met. But more important, so was his compassion. What I have learned from Nathan is tempering the wisdom with compassion. Simply knowing something is not enough. Delivery is just as, if not more, important. We work together, which has been a blessing. With each interaction, I learn something new and take away some "Nathan-ism". Also, his positive take on life is infectious. He sees the positive and shares it.

Nathan is smart, giving, compassionate, loving, funny ... the complete "friend" package. We just "get" each other. If I am headed in the wrong direction, he will point that out ... with love. That's what friends are for. Real friends see you headed in the wrong direction and step in, even if it's not what you want ... they know it's what you need.

Our friends inspire the best in us. They shore us up in all kinds of weather. They are our cheerleaders and coaches. That's Nathan in a nutshell. I have watched him with people from varying walks of life and he treats everyone the same. He is real*!*

About Toni Y. Long—I am from Dallas, Texas, and have resided in LA for over twenty years. I am an entertainment and business attorney who gets to work with and be friends with Mr. Williams. What could be better?!

NO MORE FIGHTING

I'm tired of seeing women fight! On television. On the subway. On my block. Everywhere I turn it seems I see two women of color in conflict. From the myriad of articles, posts, and comments on the Internet I know that I'm not alone. It is unfortunate that we have been bombarded with images of the "fairer" sex going gladiator. It is a sad turn for our society, and we need to turn it around quickly.

Last year, I vowed never to publicly discuss in my articles or on social media shows like *Real Housewives*, *Basketball Wives,* or *Bad Girls' Club*. I didn't want to use my platform or voice to promote the bad behavior that the casts of these shows exhibit on a weekly basis. Unfortunately, I didn't stop watching.

Now, after seeing Evelyn Lozada on *Basketball Wives* leap across a table to attack another woman who was not threatening her; I was done. To add insult to injury, on a recent episode she felt no remorse and acknowledged that at thirty-six years old (my age) she should know better, but she didn't care. For me, the nail in the coffin was when I heard a teenage girl say, "Don't make me go Evelyn on your [butt]!" With that statement, Ms. Lozada's public legacy was confirmed.

More importantly, hearing that young lady say that made me feel ashamed of myself. By supporting the show with my viewership, I was keeping it on the air for young women to see and ultimately, emulate this horrible behavior. Mindless recreation or not, I too had become a part of the problem. If no one watches then, programmers will take these programs off of the air and find alternate programming. It's ironic that positive television gets such low ratings, but we so-called positive people aren't supporting it, but will watch a grown woman cuss and fight. Yes, I'm indicting myself too.

Ms. Lozada is just one of many "women" acting far less than lady-like for ratings and fame. And, to be clear, it's not just women of color doing the fool on TV either. However, with such a dearth of images of women and men of color, I believe, there is a heightened responsibility. True, it's the networks that are programming this craziness, but they wouldn't if we didn't watch it and if there weren't women willing to do it.

But, before the masses stand in complete judgment of the ladies of the "brawl TV" shows let's take a look around us. I see women in conflict all the time. High-powered, highly educated women who definitely know better and have no cameras on them. These women might not be throwing fists, but they're doing much worse. The tongue can be a mighty sword and I've heard and seen many a woman slain for blood. Up close and personal examples of bad behavior have an even greater effect on all of us, especially our young people.

I've often said that we have to be careful what we feed our spirits. You might not think it has an affect on you, but everything you consume seeps into your sub-conscious. It begins to take residence in your psyche and can direct your actions. So, before we have more young girls "going Evelyn," sister-friends please stop fighting.

■ ■ ■

LEAVE THE GRUDGE BEHIND

In New York City, tis' the season of the best parties and celebrations of the year. Invariably, it is also the season of running into those people who have rubbed you the wrong way or gotten under your skin during the year. And if you run in the same circles it makes it even more difficult, which is why I say tis' the season to drop that grudge.

Earlier this week, one of my fabulous sister-friends and I were floating through a holiday party at a posh hotel in mid-town Manhattan. The open bar had us feeling great and we had on our holiday best. You couldn't tell us a thing until she said, "Walk the other way here comes 'Stephanie,' you know we're not speaking and I don't want to see her." At that moment, I was whisked to the other side of the room, thankfully near the seafood buffet and another bar.

For the rest of night, we played a silly game of cat and mouse making sure we avoided any contact with Stephanie.

They'd been close for many years until a falling out over the summer. The details of which are unimportant, but it was a justified rift.

"Why don't you go over to her and just speak? This makes no sense," I asked. I've never understood how people who've shared any personal relationship can be in the same room and act like they don't know each other. Everyone knows what's up, which makes you look petty and juvenile. The rift between them had passed and my sister-friend was doing great. Needless to say, we left that party early and headed to another that she was, "Sure that heffa was not going to be at."

The next day I called my sister-friend and told her that she should reach out to Stephanie to bury the hatchet. The truth was I knew she was really over the situation. Had forgiven herself and Stephanie. And, more importantly, had moved on to bigger and better things. I didn't understand why she was still carrying the remnants of the grudge around with her. I found out that she was afraid that if she were the first to make the effort that: 1) Stephanie would reject it and, 2) she'd somehow lost the battle.

"First of all, it's on Stephanie whether or not she accepts your olive branch. It's primarily for you," I advised. (We can't be responsible for how someone reacts to our actions, especially the well-intended ones.) And for that matter, who cares about the score in some mythical battle between she and Stephanie. My sister-friend was literally walking around on Cloud 9 otherwise and I thought she shouldn't take this pettiness into the holidays and New

Year. "Send that girl an e-mail and be done with it! Release this from your spirit, it'll serve you good."

She's a good student and sent her an e-mail sincerely wishing her the best. Although Stephanie didn't reply, my sister-friend felt freed from the grudge and went back to floating around. Next time we do see Stephanie, I know we won't be running from her because she truly is over it. The e-mail put the nail in the coffin and laid that battle to rest. At least for my sister-friend, which is all that mattered to me.

The holidays are about celebrating what is good in the world and being thankful for another year. Holding a grudge against someone won't serve that purpose or you well. Take a moment, release it, and leave that grudge behind you.

■ ■ ■

STAY OUT OF THE MIDDLE

One of my favorite colloquialisms from my childhood in Chicago was the phrase, "Nunya!" In one word, we were able to say an entire sentence, "It's none of your business." My auntie Gayle used to say that a lot to the other adults in the family and it always cracked me up. Today, I wish more people would say that…to themselves.

Last week, my dear sister-friend came to me perplexed about a situation between her mother and her brother. Her brother had crashed her mother's car while home for the summer from grad school. Although he was in school, her brother is in his early thirties—a grown man.

Her mother had been blowing up her phone complaining about him and threatening to put him out of the house. As you can imagine, my sister-friend's brother was not the most responsible person historically. As long as I can remember, he was always the wayward child getting into trouble with the law, having a baby out of wedlock when he was nineteen, and just a laundry list of malfeasance over the years.

My sister-friend was the older, more responsible sibling, and because of it her mother always looked to her for support. My sister-friend now has a family of her own and her own household issues she has to address on a daily basis. Still, she consistently gets caught up in the mess and drama of her family that is over 3000 miles away. I could never understand why she allowed their stress to become her own.

When she brought me this most recent situation I saw an opportunity to share with her something that had opened up in my spirit. I let her go through the whole story, which at the end of she was clearly exacerbated. She was stressed trying to figure out how to solve the riff between her mother and her brother as she had always done.

I said, "It's none of your business!"

Quickly, she replied, "Yes, it is. It's my family."

I challenged her, "But, why does that make it your business? Your mother and brother are grown. They can figure it out on their own so don't let them put you in the middle." She looked at me as if I had just told her the secret to life. Something immediately clicked in her spirit.

"Continue, I'm listening," she said. I explained that I had just experienced a similar revelation relating to some family drama. I pined over what I should do in the situation and how I should handle it. Ultimately, after praying and meditating on it my spirit told me that I didn't have to handle anything. I realized that inserting my opinion in the situation would do nothing to change it so I decided to keep it to myself.

What good would it do me to take on the drama between two adults? Absolutely none. Instead, when asked about it, I replied, "It's none of my business." In one fell swoop, I kept myself out of it and sent the message I didn't need any more information about it. Yes, it may seem cold especially when emotions are involved with loved ones you care about, but it is efficient and the best way to save yourself.

My sister-friend said, "Wow! I never thought about that, but it's so simple. You're right; it's none of my business. They need to figure it out." And they did! By staying out of it, my sister-friend reduced her stress level. She also sent a positive message to her mother and brother to fix their issues themselves. It was the best thing for everyone involved.

It caused me to think there are so many times when I have inserted myself by way of my opinion or action into a situation that was none of my business. Or, I have allowed myself to be dragged into a situation that was none of my business. It has caused me stress, and on occasion, relationships. Had I simply stayed out of it, the negative consequences of my involvement (stress, conflict, and so on) would have been completely avoided.

It is one of my newest revelations. Over the past week I have repeatedly replied, "It's none of my business." Numerous situations have been dead on arrival. Something so simple has had a huge impact for my sister-friend and for me. If you find yourself being dragged or dragging yourself into a situation that really has nothing to do with you, say to yourself, "Nunya!" And stay out the middle.

■ ■ ■

HE SHOULD CHECK HIS MOM

The overprotective, meddlesome mother-in-law is an age-old character in real life and in fiction. Most recently, as a result of reality TV the character has become a caricature in the most extreme form (Momma Dee we see you). It got me to thinking about my own family, these issues, and why any man would let this continue.

As a guy who loves and his respects his mother deeply, I completely understand and appreciate the bond between a mother and a son. However, one thing is clear in my relationship with my mother and that is I am a man, which means that I make my own decisions and run my own life. Particularly, when it comes to dating my mother stays out of my business, is respectful of my choices (whether she agrees with them or not), and respects anyone who I introduce. If I solicit advice, she gives it, but only then. That's the way it should be.

If my mother were like some other women in my family the burden on creating boundaries for her would be on me. I would never put my partner in the position that Scrappy puts Erica in or that I've seen men in my family put their wives in as a result of their overbearing mothers. Quite frankly, I don't understand why any woman would tolerate her man letting anyone disrespect her—his mother or otherwise.

The real issue is the mother does not fully want to let her son grow up and stand on his own, which in of itself is a major problem. No mother should think she is the queen of her adult son's castle. It may not go as far as Freud's Oedipus Complex, but it sure doesn't seem appropriate to me. And why any mother (or son) would want that anyway is baffling to me.

I also think it is a major character flaw when a man can't stand up to his mother on behalf of his wife or partner. He doesn't have to be disrespectful, but he should make it clear that his woman is the number one woman in his life and that his mother needs to understand her place. If she did her job when she was supposed to, then he will make choices based on his upbringing and she should trust the work she did when he was a child. Trying to run his adult life, especially his love life (whether she likes his choice in woman or not) doesn't serve anyone well.

The excuse, "That's my momma," is not a good one. Right, it's your mother and it's on you to make sure she doesn't cross the line. If you're feeling disrespected by your man's mother it's not on you to manage the situation, but on him. Is it time for your man to check his momma?

■ ■ ■

FROM MY SISTER-FRIEND, SHAUNA KAMIEL

I met Nathan approximately three years ago while working at Viacom. The story we like to tell is that we fell in love over Post-Its. He constantly needed to borrow supplies and I simply couldn't say no to such a debonair gentleman. Our love affair grew from Post-Its to cocktails with brunches, dinners, and many other good times. I felt incredibly honored when I was asked to play background in his film, Love for Passion. *I was so nervous because I am a naturally shy person, but I couldn't say no to the opportunity. I simply couldn't let Nathan down.*

Thinking about the first day of filming leads me to a funny Nathan story (one that I can tell at least). I remember Nathan told me to "come camera ready."

In retrospect I may have over did it a bit because there I was at five o'clock in the morning with my face beat honey in the restaurant, Melba's. This red-lipped shawty had arrived! From that point on there has been an ongoing joke of my background acting skills. I don't mean to brag, but I've been referred to as the Meryl Streep of background performers. I'm just waiting for the Academy to create a new category.

It is so hard to pinpoint the best piece of advice that Nathan has ever given. He is a constant, and I do mean constant, source of positivity. One conversation that sticks out to me is when I texted him asking if I was crazy for considering law school. We all know how expensive education is nowadays, and some of you may be privy to the fact that it is difficult for new lawyers to find a job. Nathan's response was "Why not?" It was all so simple to him. Why not follow your dreams? Why not aspire to be great? Isn't that what we are put on this earth to do? With that very fitting Nathan response, I suddenly felt comforted and inspired.

This past August, Nathan gave me a birthday shout out in which he described our friendship as "full and beautiful." After reading that message, I've held the "full and beautiful" standard up to many of my other relationships. Now we know there can only be one Nathan Hale Williams, however I have no problem letting people know that he is one of my favorite people in the whole world, and they should aspire to be like him. It's not just the accolades that make him great, it's the joy he brings into the lives of others. Nathan is a girl's best friend because he creates a home in your heart. That place is where you are comfortable enough to share your dreams and fears without being judged.

About Shauna Kamiel—A dreamer and doer, Shauna carries the legacy of those before her striving to live here life purposefully. She's a philanthropist, sister, friend, sister-friend, and last, but not least Nathan's party girl.

SANTA NEEDS TO CALM DOWN

Tis' the season to lose your mind! I love the holidays, but not the extreme consumerism that has taken the place of the true reason for the season. For me, it's about spending time with family and friends, eating well, and celebrating another year of life. For many, it is about the excess that comes with the gift giving aspect. Case in point, people foregoing time with their families on Thanksgiving to camp out on Black Friday. It's gotten ridiculous.

Last week, my sister-friend who has two young children both under the age of five and I were talking about her Christmas shopping. Granted, she and her husband do very well, but when she told me her Christmas shopping budget was $10,000.00 I almost fell out of my chair. And that was just for the kids. "Have you lost your damn mind," I had to ask?

Believe it or not, my sister-friend didn't think that was extravagant. I couldn't believe she would even consider spending that kind of money on kids who would never remember any of the gifts. I don't know about you, but I certainly don't remember anything under the age of five except a few glimpses here and there. I most definitely don't remember my Christmas gifts, which were probably all broken by March anyway.

"What will they have to look forward to if you're spending this kind of money on them now," I questioned? Unfortunately, my sister-friend is just a representation of the collective insanity that has become the benchmark for Christmas. People go into debt that will take them years to pay off for gifts. For what? It's a temporary, material high that fades when the bills show up. And even if you don't go into debt, is it really the gift that is important or the giver?

But this type of excess is celebrated all around us. Beyoncé reportedly bought Jay-Z the most expensive watch in the world estimated between $3-5 Million dollars for his birthday. That followed her gift of a jet for Father's Day. With a new $50 Million-dollar contract, Beyoncé can afford it, but is it really that serious. Don't get me started on those *Sweet 16* shows and the lunacy displayed there.

It's not about the gifts, but about the message it sends. Placing so much importance on the material discredits not only the point of celebrating Christmas, but also when it comes to children it doesn't send the right value message. My best friends who are both well off have the more sensible approach. Their kids still have unopened birthday and

Christmas gifts hidden away because they get so much. "They can get them next year, they already have too many toys and things," they've both been known to say.

As I have grown up, I've received fewer gifts, but that has no affect on my pure enjoyment for the season. What I remember most is the time spent with family; it's even what I remember most from my childhood. I can tell you about card games and funny situations better than I can about actual presents I received. I think we all need to take a pause and tell Santa Claus to calm down.

I LOOK TO YOU—SPIRIT

*"After all my strength is gone,
in you I can be strong."*

—Robert Kelly

*"Alone time is when I distance myself from
the voices of the world so I can hear my own."*

—Oprah

TIME TO REJUVENATE YOUR SPIRIT

Immediately following the Fourth of July, I was broken down. I was so tired that I could barely see straight. The pace of a dynamic life can get to you and it has a direct affect on your spirit. Even I, the eternal optimist, was in a bad mood. My body was also physically reacting to my exhaustion via a cold sore and a cough. Thankfully, I'd scheduled some time in my hometown of Chicago. If you know the feeling, it is probably time for some spirit rejuvenation.

On normal days, I'm able to go to gratitude and create a great day. I truly believe we have all of the power to make every day a jubilant one if we focus on what is good in our lives and not the opposite. A focus on our abundance and not our lack helps keep things in perspective.

The phrase, "mind, body and spirit" is nothing, but the truth. It's the trinity of our beings, and when any of those three things is out of sync the other two are affected. We all lead ridiculously busy lives with the pressures pulling on our energy at a non-stop pace. Particularly women who have to juggle, motherhood, career, wife, and friendships; there are so many demands for your time and attention.

Yesterday, I heard a statement on PBS' *Frontline* that, "We are wired to put other people's needs before ours." I've said this before, but that is backward thinking. You certainly can't be one hundred percent for someone else without first being one hundred percent for yourself. While you're running around exhausted, overwhelmed, and stressed you are not only doing yourself a disservice you are not giving your all to the people that count on you.

For this reason, I think that every woman (and man) should take a moment to recharge at least every three months. I say every three months because it goes with the natural flow of time. And, by recharge, I don't just mean a trip to a manicurist or one massage. A healthy recharge is across several days of relaxation, meditation, and some self-pampering. Paying attention to yourself in a way you don't often get to do.

So many women who have multiple responsibilities can't imagine finding the time for this type of exercise. However, if you look at it as a spiritual necessity, and not a luxury you can make time. Find ways to put those responsibilities on pause or at least greatly reduce them. Send the kids to your mom's house for three days. Tell your husband you're checking into a hotel for two days, and not to call you. Take consecutive days off from work. And during those days focus on no one else, but you.

For me, it means coming home to Chicago where my retired mother is happy to wait on me and take care of all of the things I usually handle. I don't make a schedule. I take baths (when was the last time you took a long bath) and I don't answer the phone, or respond to anyone who stresses me out. It's much more therapeutic than a vacation because I literally have no obligations except to get up, eat and sleep. Everything else is gravy. It does the trick every time; and after I am ready to keep moving into my destiny with a rejuvenated spirit.

If you're feeling overwhelmed, over worked, exhausted, and spiritually spent it is probably time for you to take an extended break from the world. Trust me, the world will be fine without you for a couple of days. You owe it to yourself to rejuvenate your spirit.

■ ■ ■

A NEW SEASON, A NEW YOU

If you're anything like me and you live in a climate that has four seasons you get excited when the spring comes. It is cold and barren in the winter and the coming of the spring signals renewal and rebirth. One of the most common activities associated with the arrival of spring is cleaning.

The spring is the time when you go through your closets and throw out old unusable things. You may donate the items or just simply toss them in the garbage. You wax floors, clean the refrigerator, plant flowers, and plants. Whatever ritual you follow; spring is about a fresh start.

The same holds true for relationships. One of my sister-friends had a rough winter. She found herself stuck in a relationship that was not meeting her needs. Luckily, she had the sense enough to end the relationship a couple of weeks ago. She is certainly not alone as many "winter romances" are ending across the country.

"Winter romances" are a common phenomenon. No one wants to be alone on cold winter nights or out searching so you settle for something that you know doesn't cut it to survive the winter. But these relationships usually don't make it to the first day of spring.

Over the weekend, my sister-friend and I were talking about her recently ended relationship and the upcoming spring/summer season. We were discussing our plans for work and travel. I told her I was taking the time this spring to shed some baggage and I had no intention of dating anyone seriously.

My sister-friend made the good point of always remaining open (advice I had given her in the past). While I agree that you can never close yourself off to love, I challenged her to take a moment to rediscover who she is when standing alone. Take some time for reflection and spiritual rebirth. That way, when the summer hits she is fresh and renewed.

I went on to explain that I think it's very healthy to use the change in seasons for self-reflection and cleansing. For single people (and people in relationships as well), it is a good way to make sure you're checked into your own spirit. An internal spring-cleaning that I don't believe can be accomplished within the confines of a new relationship. You have to go it alone!

My sister-friend is always interested in being her best and so she accepted my challenge. We have both agreed to reexamine who we are at our core. Setting goals and rediscovering what makes us tick and assessing areas of our personalities that can use some work. We're doing a spiritual tune-up, if you will. A spring-cleaning of the spirit.

As my sister-friend pointed out, this was very new age of me and a bit out of character. As I have gotten older, I've learned to embrace these "ohm" moments as necessary to my growth and extremely helpful. Particularly, if the ultimate goal is to be in a loving, long-lasting, and supportive relationship the best way to find that is to be able to provide that to someone yourself. You can't do that if your own spirit needs some work.

We have begun the internal work with daily prayer and meditation. We both pray and meditate regularly already, but during this spring season our intention is focused on renewal and rebirth. Even the most evolved people can use a spiritual check-up and cleansing from time to time. We're also doing activities that stimulate our spirits and bring us joy.

The spring is an opportunity to shed the heaviness of the winter and the wounds of any failed past relationships that you're carrying around. I challenge you to focus on your own spirit this spring with the goal of finding a new you! The relationship you have with yourself is by far the most important relationship in your life. If that relationship isn't working, no other relationship will work either. So, cheers to a new season and a new you.

■ ■ ■

HAPPINESS IS YOURS

As we embark on a new year, so many of us make resolutions to lose weight, stop smoking, go to church, stick to a budget, and the annual list goes on. About two years ago, I decided I was no longer going to make resolutions each new-year and instead develop mantras that I would focus on living my life by throughout the year. Last year, one such mantra was to find joy and happiness in every situation—good or bad.

I didn't know it then, but I couldn't have picked a better mantra for 2011 because I surely encountered a lot of difficult situations. To put it lightly, 2011 was rough. Needless to say, I was happy to usher in a new year and optimistic about the possibilities. More importantly, I learned a valuable lesson that there *is* joy in every situation and I'm in control of it.

Last week, I was having year-end cocktails with one of my sister-friends who also had a tough year. Her marriage had suffered some serious blows and she was unhappy at work. By the holiday season, she was at wits end and really was just ready to end the year.

"Girl, what's the matter," I asked (already knowing the answer)?

"Chile, it's just been one ole' year," she sullenly replied as she sipped her margarita. "Yes, but you look like you've been through World War III," I quipped.

"It feels like I have, you've had a tough year too!"

And, as I said, she was right. My year was challenging. However, I went on to explain how setting that mantra for myself at the top of the year had helped me through the most difficult times. True, my circumstances weren't the most ideal, but what I'd discovered is that I had the power to make myself happy no matter what.

I shared with her my discovery, "Happiness is a choice, not a gift. By going to gratitude and focusing on the things that were good in my life I was able to tackle the crazy stuff with a smile. Sure, I didn't like it, but wasn't it enough that I had to deal with it? I refused to let mere temporary situations affect my overall happiness. I often found myself saying, 'it is what is.' And once I stopped going against the flow of the universe I was able to accept the situation, try to move passed it and still stay happy."

"Alright, Deepak Chopra, I know you've been on this spirituality kick, but you can calm down. It's not that simple," she half-joked. "I had to deal with [her husband] cheating on me, my job being crazy, money wasn't right… it was *a lot*!!!"

"So, what?! [Stuff] happens, but you made the choice to focus on the bad parts. You made the choice to be miserable. You made the choice not to accept it for what it was deal with it and move on." I was not diminishing the severity of her issues. Instead, I was encouraging the power of her spirit to make the choice to find joy in her life in spite of those issues.

One thing about friendship is that you have to know when to pull back because no matter what you do the other person isn't quite ready to receive the love you're giving. Unfortunately, that was the case with my sister-friend last week. She wasn't in the place to hear me. I will try again when she's bounced back a bit because I do hope she discovers what I discovered.

We create our own reality and existence. If we say we're miserable and focus on the bad, then we're miserable. Conversely, if we focus on the good in our life and proclaim joy, then we become that too. My hope is that as you begin a new year that you go to gratitude in all situations, especially the bad ones. And remember that happiness is yours.

■ ■ ■

LIVING & LOVING IN THE NOW

I was watching my sister-friend (in my head), Oprah on her series, *Life Class with Deepak Chopra*, as they discussed living in the "now." For the past five years, I've been reading about and practicing the exercise of being solely in the present moment. I concede that it is no easy task and it takes a lot of practice, however, the effort toward doing practicing it has changed my life dramatically. With that said, I haven't actively applied it to love, but it should be.

Over the weekend, I was at a party with one of my sister-friends and her ex-boyfriend came into the party. Although they've been broken up for over a year, my sister-friend's ex still has feelings for her and somehow manages to get her caught up every time they interact. My other sister-friend who was at the party is single and is on the hunt for a man. She's so consumed with finding a new relationship she starts fantasizing about every guy that speaks to her.

Although my sister-friends are on opposite ends of the love spectrum I believe they share the same problem. (A problem that I've been known to have myself as well). Neither one of them is loving in their present moment. My one sister-friend allows her ex-man to take her back to a past moment in her love journey forcing her to revisit the drama and pain of their relationship. While my other sister-friend is so caught up in the future that she comes off desperate instead of living in the now.

Both love scenarios lead to spiritual conflict for the same reason that living in the past or being overly concerned about the future can cause turmoil. You can't change the past and you can't predict the future. The only true reality is the moment that exists now. In that moment, my one sister-friend is no longer in a relationship with her ex and so there's no reason to rehash the past, especially if its preventing one or both of them from truly moving forward.

Conversely, my other sister-friend's preoccupation with her future dream man makes her less desirable to guys who actually are interested. Her desperation manifests itself in the way she reacts to every little thing they do. She laughs too hard at their jokes. She gets jealous too quickly if they're speaking to someone else. In her head, she's already planning her wedding on the first date. It ultimately ruins the process and never works out.

My advice to both of them and all of us is the same. Start loving in the now. If you're in a relationship, then maybe you need to stop reminiscing about how things were (for better or worse) and appreciate how they are now. Only then can you deal with any love issues between you and your mate. You might also need to be realistic if you're waiting on circumstances to change. Your current circumstances are what they are and the only way to deal with them is to embrace them in this moment.

I truly believe we make life and love much harder than either needs to be. It can often be attributed to the fact that we're either living in the past or the future. The best way to live the life you've imagined and love the way you dreamed is to live and love in the now.

■ ■ ■

YOU ARE WORTHY OF LOVE

Thankfully, I learned early in life that I could be my best friend and my biggest enemy. I've chosen to get out of my own way and be a friend one hundred percent of the time. Whenever the enemy side starts feeding my spirit bad information about me the friend jumps in to let me know how great I am. The same is true about love; many of us don't truly feel we are worthy of it.

I had to do a "friend-tervention" with one of my sister-friends a few weeks ago. She was so distraught because another bad relationship had ended. As she lamented on the loss of the relationship, I had to recount for her all of the crazy stuff the guy had done to her. Like the comedian Sommore jokes, this dude should have come with a warning label detailing all of his "side effects."

It then dawned on me that this was a pattern for her. And there had been plenty of decent guys that had approached her in the past—some that I had introduced to her. However, she consistently was attracted to men that mistreated her. She always found something wrong with the good guys and gravitated toward the deadbeats.

I said to her, "You are worthy of love!" A very simple statement, however, it struck a profound note with my sister-friend who immediately began to cry. It hadn't occurred to me that the core reason why she continuously allowed herself to be in destructive relationships was because she didn't feel worthy of love. Somewhere deep down she felt she deserved to be treated badly.

I could empathize with her because I too had suffered from severe insecurity and low self-esteem. As a result, I often allowed myself to get into bad situations because I didn't think I was worth more. It wasn't until I began to love myself fully that I stopped inviting destruction into my life.

During our discussion, I couldn't help, but think about the countless people who do not consciously believe they are worthy of love. Nothing could be farther from the truth. Love is the most powerful force in the universe and it is our birthright. And there is nothing about love that is destructive or harmful.

With that in mind, it is very easy to decipher between a good and bad relationship. It has helped me to maintain outstanding friendships and relationships. As well, it has pushed me to move on from toxic relationships with people who did not love themselves or me.

God/the universe doesn't want us to be in conflict, which ultimately is the absence of a love in a situation. Instead, love should be at the center of all we do. If you are conscious of it you know when it is and when it isn't.

Like my sister-friend, life has led too many us to believe bad information about ourselves. This incorrect thinking leads into situations that are destructive and harmful. But no matter what bad information you've believed one fact will never change and that is you are worthy of love.

■ ■ ■

SPIRITUAL COMPATIBILITY

Last week, the world went to church—black Baptist style—during the funeral of my favorite entertainer and idol, Whitney Houston. For many, it was the first time they'd experience a "homegoing" in that manner. For me, it was what I expected from Whitney's family and I thought it was pitch perfect. It did raise a debate though on spiritual practices. It made me wonder whether people question their spiritual compatibility when entering into a new relationship.

To be clear, I'm not merely speaking about religion because I don't consider myself religious although I go to church regularly. Over the years, I've met many "religious" people who needed to work on their spirits. I think we all can relate. Many of those religious people give religion a bad name by doing evil and injustice in the name of religion. No, I'm talking about spirituality, which is a different and loftier concept.

Last year, I had one of my sister-friends over who'd recently started dating a guy who practiced Buddhism. She is a devout and faithful Christian, which made her wrestle with the idea of getting into a serious relationship with a Buddhist. It troubled her because it was really her only concern. Otherwise, the guy she was dating was exceptional.

"Well, are you spiritually compatible," I asked?

She replied, "Clearly, we're not." She misunderstood my question. I wasn't asking did they follow the same religion or religious practices, but rather when it came down to the way they both looked at the world—their spirituality and faith—were those beliefs congruent? It made her think beyond mere nomenclature and go to the root of true spirituality.

My pastor often cites that many of the world's religions taken at their core believe the same fundamental things about life and the way you live it. Jesus isn't much different than Buddha, and so forth. The golden rule runs throughout most of the world's religions. I encouraged her to have a talk with him about his faith, why he practices Buddhism, and the fundamentals of the practice.

Personally, I'd been in relationships with people who would deem themselves Christians, but spiritually we weren't compatible. Our life views were diametrically different and we didn't speak the same spiritual language although we shared the same religion. From my experience,

I knew there was more to the story than the surface of a religious title. Plus, I'd encountered many Buddhists along the way and found myself agreeing with the great majority of what they had to say about life.

My sister-friend took my advice and they had a month-long education on Christianity and Buddhism. He also wanted to experience Christianity from her perspective, as his previous encounters had not been good. In turn, she learned more about Buddhism and accompanied him to see his practice. They both discovered that there were more similarities than differences in their beliefs and spiritual language. The exercise actually bonded them even further and they'll be getting married this fall.

It worked out for my sister-friend because she and her fiancée are spiritually compatible. However, it could go the other way if you're not, especially if spirituality/religion is important to one person and not the other. Along with questions about kids, finances, and sex I encourage you to also ask, "Are we spiritually compatible?"

■ ■ ■

CREATE YOUR JOY

"There's nothing I don't love about my life. It's a struggle, but that's why they call it life." —Dr. Maya Angelou. There is so much power in that statement that it has pushed me toward an understanding of the control I have over my life. I wish more people realized that they create either their own joy or their own misery.

We all have that friend who no matter what day it is or what has happened something is wrong. One of my sister-friends is that friend for me. She is constantly complaining about one thing or another. Seemingly, she is never in a good mood. Over the years, I've tried to be a supportive friend by providing some encouragement and positive energy.

Recently, we were speaking and I was my usual optimistic self. She questioned whether it was genuine or an act. The fact that she even asked the question let me know that she didn't know me well despite our years of friendship. It also let me know that she did not realize her choices.

"Sure, I have problems and issues, but I choose not to focus on those and instead on the things that are going well in my life," I said. I went onto explain that whenever I am feeling bad I practice the act of listing the things I'm grateful for either in my mind or writing them down. It is a technique I acquired during an extended depressive state and one that works without fail.

By focusing on gratitude, I can't help, but to change the way I feel about a particular (temporary) circumstance. And if I need more I do something that makes me happy like listen to my favorite song or dance or call my mom. Once I realized I had the power over my own feelings and emotions; it's rare that I have a bad day. The revelation of my personal power over my spirit was one of the best "aha" moments I have ever had.

As you can imagine, she wasn't buying what I was selling. You'd be surprised (or maybe you wouldn't) how many people would rather be miserable than to accept that they are in control of their life. Outwardly, you would never know that I was having difficulties in almost every aspect of my life last year. Instead, I chose to find my joy in every circumstance and it made it so much easier.

I challenged my sister-friend to do the exercise of writing down the things that she is grateful for the next time she's feeling down. I'm not sure if she will do it, but you definitely should give it a try. Instead of being miserable create your joy.

■ ■ ■

THE HEALING SEASON

I'm not going to lie 2012 has been a rough year. I know many people share that sentiment as I know most of my friends do. For me, the year started with the loss of my favorite entertainer, Whitney Houston, then one of my favorite aunts (I only have two) and ended with the loss of my friend, celebrity make-up artist Ross Burton. And, of course, the entire nation and world is mourning the recent tragedy that occurred in Newtown, Connecticut. On so many levels I think we are all in need of a collective healing.

Not one for ever wallowing in sadness, I am super excited about the holidays because what better time to celebrate life, make wrongs right, and be hopeful for a brighter future. Yes, leading up to next week has been trying, but as we get closer to it the more I am able to focus on the rejuvenation that the holiday season can bring. I'm taking the opportunity to do some things to recharge my spirit and truly embrace the beauty of the season.

Here are some ways to heal a troubled spirit that work for me and that I am currently practicing.

1. **Meditation**. I have been trying to meditate for years, but thanks to Deepak Chopra and Oprah giving away a *21-Day Meditation Challenge* for free I have been meditating more frequently and it really works. I encourage you to try it if you've never done it before. Don't give up if it doesn't work so well the first time. I'm told it takes twenty-one days to create a habit.
2. **Journaling**. Here's another one that I just hadn't been able to get into in the past, but I've been journaling and it has completely been a cheap form of therapy. With journaling you can say what's really on your mind. We all possess the ability to heal ourselves within our spirits and sometimes you just have to write it out to see it.
3. **Help somebody**. I often find when I call a friend and ask, "How can I help you today?" I always feel better. It truly puts things in perspective when you help someone and put your spirit in a posture of service. With so much loss this year, including those affected by Sandy, there is always someone who stands in need. You probably don't have to look too far outside of your family and friends.

4. **Forgive someone and apologize**. I have often said in this column that forgiveness is for you. It is crucial to healing a wounded spirit and broken heart. Even if you don't contact the person, still forgive them in your heart. And then apologize if you can. "Apologizing doesn't mean you're wrong; it just means you value your relationships more than your ego." – Will Smith
5. **Celebrate**. I come from a family that knows how to party. Don't forget to celebrate all that you have and the people in your life. Nothing says the holidays and joy to me more than being able to celebrate and party with the people that mean the most to me.

I can't think of a better gift you can give yourself than putting your spirit in a position to heal. It will do wonders for you and those around you.

■ ■ ■

FORGIVENESS IS FOR YOU

Everyone makes mistakes. Everyone! Some mistakes have greater consequences and implications than others, but if you're human you've made both big and small ones. For that reason, it baffles me how so many people refuse to forgive others for their mistakes.

One of my sister-friends recently remarried after being single for about seven years. Her first marriage ended in a very bitter and contentious divorce. She had not spoken to her ex-husband in almost five years since the divorce was finalized. He had been pretty awful during their marriage with infidelity and some verbal abuse.

About a week before she got married, her ex-husband sent her an e-mail wishing her congratulations and apologizing for his wrongdoing. He acknowledged that he was immature and his mistreatment of her was not what she deserved. Also, he asked to meet with her some time so he could apologize in person. Although he made it clear that this was not an attempt to get her back expressing his respect of her fiancé.

"Why the hell would I meet with him?" she asked when we met to discuss the e-mail. My sister-friend went on to recount all of the vile and horrible things her ex-husband had done and said during the marriage, especially in the divorce. He had fought her on every aspect of the settlement refusing to give her a dime. He definitely was a piece of work and put her through hell.

The difficult time my sister-friend had with her ex-husband was often a barrier for new relationships. In terms of baggage, she had a full set of Louis Vuitton luggage. Thankfully, she met a wonderful man who was willing to love her through her issues and she got over most of it. With that said, I never believed she had full closure because she had not forgiven her ex-husband.

I decided to push her a bit and asked, "Maybe meeting with him is exactly what you need to do before you get married again." She couldn't understand what one had to do with the other. I explained that she needed to fully close that emotional chapter and the only way she was going to be able to move forward in a brand-new marriage was if she left the pain of the last one in the past.

"Give him a chance to apologize, listen to him, and then forgive him!" I encouraged her to push herself to let it all go, look at him with clean eyes, and a clean heart. "That [brotha] ain't changed…I know him," she retorted. She wasn't having it, which was an indication that she hadn't fully moved passed her hurt feelings. So, I knew she *had* to meet with him and she had to begin the process of forgiveness.

The key misconception she was making was that forgiving him was about him. In fact, the forgiveness I was encouraging was for her and her spirit. By holding on to the hurt and the memories of the bad acts she was disabling her spirit from its full expression. At the mention of his name she would recoil. If you're holding something that powerful and negative in your spirit you can't possibly be living your best life.

As an example, I reminded her of several instances with her fiancé that were manifestations of the hurt she harbored. He'd do something that reminded her of her ex-husband and she'd jump to the conclusion that her fiancé was doing something similar. In every instance she had misread the situation and ended up having to apologize. She certainly didn't want to take that into the marriage.

Then, I went in for the kill, and said to her, "The forgiveness that you refuse will be the forgiveness that you seek. When you have compassion for others when they make mistakes you will receive compassion when you make yours. And you will continue to make mistakes."

She replied, "Damn, that's deep!"

Yes, it is deep, but it is also the truth. By letting her heart house even just a bit of negative energy or ill will prevented it from being completely filled with love and positive energy. Forgiving her ex-husband would open up that space in her heart and spirit for goodness. It seems to be an esoteric concept, but its simple physics—two things can't occupy the same space at the same time.

Reluctantly, she took my advice and met with him. And they had a good time. He apologized and she listened. Once she listened to him and opened her spirit for understanding, she realized he had changed. We all can change and her ex-husband did the work to do it. Most importantly, she started the process of forgiveness and went into her second marriage leaving a lot of that Louis Vuitton behind.

We all have make mistakes and have issues with the people in our lives. Holding a grudge never does anyone any good. It just perpetuates and prolongs a negative experience. And if you're in the position to accept an apology and forgive someone do it because the forgiveness is for you!

■ ■ ■

A COLLECTIVE HEALING

We've all lost our minds! I realized I had gone bonkers after reviewing my chosen night of TV programming. From *Basketball Wives* to *Real Housewives of Beverly Hills* to *The Bad Girls Club*, aside from the US Open, I had chosen chaos to entertain me. No matter which of the franchises I was watching it was the same script, different cast—senseless conflict and dysfunctional relationships. All for our viewing pleasure.

Ironically, I don't watch the news to avoid all of the doom and gloom that our news media seems to focus on, especially on the local evening news. Without fail, the lead story reminds us that we're not safe, we're all broke (except for those Wall Street guys), and that the world is coming to an end. Equally, I gave up the addiction I had developed during the Obama campaign to "liberal" cable news. I was determined not to let the news destroy my happy.

(But instead I watch Tami Roman throw drinks and fists at other women).

I find even greater irony in the fact that most responsible adults protect and monitor what our children consume for entertainment. We do this because we know the affect media can have on a child's development and perception of him or herself. There's something about the power of media that has the ability shape our beliefs about our world and ourselves. Yet, as adults, we consistently consume things that perpetuate the most negative aspects about us as a society and as individuals.

To that end, I really do believe all of this negative consumption is taking a toll on our relationships. We're being fed the wrong information on how to conduct ourselves in our personal and intimate relationships. We look at our President who tries to conduct himself in a civil manner as being weak, not a fighter, or tough enough. And we're so combative and destructive in our own relationships that we forget that being civil and kind is a sign of strength not weakness.

It was on my spirit this past week, in particular after having several of my sister-friends come to me with various issues within their relationships. Some issues in the grand scheme of things will prove to be minor bumps while others may add up to be deal-breakers. Miraculously, I was at a loss of advice for many of them so I gave my support and my friendship. I have learned some times you need to just be there for someone without any feedback.

With that said, I couldn't help but to contemplate everything and try to make some sense of it all for myself. It wasn't until watching television last night that it dawned on me. As a society…as a world…we are in need of a collective healing. We are consistently bombarded with so much negative information that it's difficult to find the sanity in your day-to-day living. Thus, it forces us to act in a way that is contrary to our life's goals or the standard by which we know how to conduct our lives.

Husbands and wives are fighting because of their money and infidelity. Brothers and sisters aren't talking because of a simple misunderstanding. Friends are ending great friendships due to a misspoken word. The reason why we're watching the crap we're watching is because we're living these shows every day and we want to feel better about it. "At least someone is crazier than I am," we think.

Instead, we should be working to mend our relationships and keep the viable ones strong. A consistent problem in all of those "girl fight" shows is the lack of communication. The only way you're going to be able to save, maintain, or grow a relationship is through proper and frequent communication. We often fail to communicate our feelings to the people who mean the most to us.

Communication is the first step to healing our wounds. And from the looks of it our country is a collection of the walking wounded. Healing also continues with forgiveness. You must first forgive yourself for your contribution to the problem (and if there's a problem both people contributed to it). And then forgive your spouse, sister, friend, or co-worker for their actions. It always bothers me when people say, "I don't think I can forgive her for this." As I say, the forgiveness you refuse will be the forgiveness you seek.

Then, we need to do what they don't do on those television shows—move forward from a place of love. I pray each day that God opens my spirit and guides all of my actions from a place of love. I don't always succeed one hundred percent, but when that is your goal it is very difficult to encounter the constant turmoil that we've come to know as "normal." When love is a priority, then those little devils: ego, pride, vanity, arrogance, and so on have no power to live in your spirit or your relationships.

Just as we protect what our children consume, we must also protect what we consume. Moreover, we need to begin a collective healing to rebuild our society to a point where those shows no longer have a place. But it starts on the micro level with our own personal relationships. Let's begin to save us all by saving the ones closest to us and ourselves. It is the first step to a much-needed collective healing.

■ ■ ■

THE WIZ: A SPIRITUAL JOURNEY

"There's a feeling here inside that I cannot hide and I know I've tried, but it's turning me around...I think the feeling is fear." The lyrics to "Soon as I Get Home" from *The Wiz* set the stage for Dorothy's journey through Oz. The entire African-American adaptation of *The Wizard of Oz* chronicles the spiritual journey of finding yourself in the midst of chaos.

Earlier this week, one of my sister-friends found herself at a crossroads in her career and her personal life. She was feeling displaced in the crazy world that is New York City, and like Dorothy, felt as if she was "drowning." I pulled out my copy of the original Broadway soundtrack and played for her my favorite song from the musical, "Be A Lion."

As I lip synced to Stephanie Mills, I know my sister-friend thought I was crazy until she began to pay attention to the words of the song. She is encouraging the Cowardly Lion that he has always been a lion and that there was no need for him to *try* to be because he always was.

With that, my sister-friend began to get the point, and, for me too, it opened a new understanding of the musical's message. One of the things that perplexes us is our pursuit of so much in life, love, and our careers. Instead of just being, we are constantly in search of some magic that will transform our lives. As *The Wiz* explains, our joy lives inside of us and there is no need to search for it.

Upon the killing of Evilene, the cast sings, "Everybody Rejoice," celebrating their newfound freedom from the evils of the world personified by the Wicked Witch. The song reminds us "the sun is shining just for us." Freedom truly is a state of mind because all any of the characters had to do was pull the sprinkler system and Evilene would have disintegrated. Dorothy finally got the courage and everyone was free even though they always had the ability to do the same.

Further along in the musical, Glenda tells Dorothy "If you believe in your heart you'll know that no one can change the path you must go." Deep down, we all know that nothing will come to pass if you don't first believe that it will. The anxiety that my sister-friend was feeling was a result from a lack of belief that her desired outcome would happen. In fact, the challenges and obstacles in her life made her lose her belief in herself.

In the finale, Dorothy sings about "Home" and in the original version Glenda tells her one of my favorite mantras, "You've always had the power, my dear. You just had to learn it for yourself." As she looks back on her journey through Oz she realizes home lives inside of her spirit and that no matter what she can never be separated from it. She clicks her heels, and then she goes back home.

I wish I could say that I always got the messages of *The Wiz* before the other night. My intention was just to play one song for my sister-friend. The discovery that occurred took both of our understandings of our own journeys through life to another level. Truly, everything we need and want we already have. There is no need to search for courage, freedom, or home.

■ ■ ■

LET IT SHINE

If you're a Christian, you probably grew up singing that song in church, "This little light of mine, I'm going to let it shine. Let it shine. Let it shine." My heart melts when I see the toddlers sing that today at my church. Such a simple song with a huge meaning—God/the Universe has given you a light to shine and you should let it.

I love to watch children play, specifically my Godchildren, Jayden and Elliot. They are discovering the world one leaf, one spider, and one ice cream cone at a time. It is wonderful to see them attack life with such a brilliant and pure light.

It is the main reason why I hate to see some parents and adults do things to dim that light by forgetting kids are kids and not adults. I think the worst thing you can do to a child is dim the natural light that shines within him or her. It is equally disheartening for me to see adults dim their own lights, especially for someone else.

One of my sister-friends who I'm not that close with, but I have known for years has always been a vibrant person. She's the type of woman who wears those outfits that borderline outrageous, but work for her because she has the personality. I have always admired her zeal for life and her indifference to what other people thought. She did her thing no matter what!

It was her enigmatic personality that always made everyone want to be around her. She was definitely someone you wanted on the list at your party as you could count on her to do something ridiculously fun. We all loved her just the way she was.

I hadn't seen her in a couple of years and we both ended up at a mutual friend's birthday party. Turns out, she had gotten married and had a baby. I was so happy for her and wanted to know everything about her husband and her new life. I offered to grab us some cocktails so we could sip while we caught up. She said she no longer drank alcohol. It was a shocker to me because she could drink a linebacker under the table. But I do understand people evolve and didn't think much of it.

When I returned with my gimlet in hand and her Sprite we sat down to shoot the breeze. As she told me about her day-to-day life I felt like I was talking to a complete stranger. This couldn't be the wild and crazy girl that I'd known for years. Instead, some demure Stepford Wife had invaded her body. Then, I noticed how she was dressed—floral print dress, two-inch pumps, and pearls. Wow!

As she continued talking about her life, I felt like I was in an episode of Charlie Brown because all I heard was "womp, womp, womp!" I was stunned! Don't get me wrong; I know people do change. But this was like Snooki becoming Mother Theresa; people don't change that much! More importantly, I was getting bored. The interesting, hip, and live on the edge girl I knew was clearly gone and I was counting the moments when I could break away from her.

Then, I said it! I was probably out of line, but I had to do it. I asked, "So, what gives? You're a completely different person than what I remember you to be." At first, she was taken aback by the question. She paused for a moment and saw an opportunity to talk. She told me that her husband was really conservative—a Republican—and how over the course of their relationship he'd made "suggestions" on how she should conduct herself. He had intentions on running for office.

I could tell she was unhappy with this change, but she clearly loved her husband and child. My question was, "Who did he think he was marrying?"

Her response, "He says he saw my potential past all of the other stuff." I was heated! All that "other stuff" was what made her special; it was her light.

Of course, I went on to encourage her to let her light shine. Otherwise, she was going to be miserable for the rest of her life. I asked, "Do you even like pearls?" She gave me that smile that reads, "Hell no!" My goal was not to interfere in her relationship because she had clearly made some choices. I did, however, want to encourage her to seek a way that she could be more of herself and let her true light shine.

I don't know what happened with my sister-friend after that birthday party. I haven't seen her since. I pray that she is becoming more secure in who she really is at the core and allowing herself space to be that person within the confines of her marriage. Not only is she doing herself a disservice; her husband is missing out on a truly awesome woman.

I see so many women dim their lights for men and nothing upsets me more. Don't play dumb! Don't play conservative, if you're not! Don't play anything—be yourself! If a man is looking for you to mute your music, then he's not the man for you. You can only be someone else for so long before your true self comes out. And it's usually too late then. It's best for you to stay true to the light God gave you and let it shine!

Wishing you love and ceaseless joy!

A NOTE AFTERWORD FROM MOMMA J

February 22nd was the beginning of a love affair that transformed into a relationship between a child and parent that has now grown into the best of friends.

My son, Nathan is an amazing person who only needs a parent for some instruction and love. Love is the most important ingredient. That is what God intended for parents to provide to their children. And to introduce the child to God's light, spirit, and love.

Knowing these things would provide him with direction and sustain him much better than I could was my job. As a result, it has helped to create in Nathan a loving, caring individual who respects others with the love of God. His advice is always filled with spiritual guidance to assist the receiver with finding their own light. He is a blessing! And I mean that sincerely.

With all of the good things I see he is doing I know the chosen name Nathan, which means "a gift from God" was the best name for my son. He has been my gift and will be yours if you allow him. He is amazing and someone to be experienced. He is truly the best in the east, west, south, and north! I hope you've enjoyed as well as learned from the great lessons and advice from my amazingly wonderful son, Nathan aka The Girl's Best Friend.

ACKNOWLEDGMENTS

I did a very long acknowledgment section for my novel, *Ladies Who Lunch & Love* so I won't do one here. I have been tremendously blessed by the family and friends in my life. To all of you, without you I wouldn't be able to climb mountains daily and do it with so much joy. You are the wind beneath my wings and the light in my times of darkness. I love you beyond words; and I know you know who you are. Thank you!

A special thank you to my fabulous and fierce sister-friends who lent a note to this book. And those whose lives inspired my column. Thank you for allowing me to use your experiences as a teaching tool for my readers and me.

Finally, I have to thank my dear friend and love, *the* Mr. Emil Wilbekin. Sir, our friendship and love have grown so much over the years and it is truly one that I cherish deeply. Thank you for giving me the opportunity to write this column. It literally changed my life. I'll love you and be grateful to you forever. Thank you, *Essence magazine,* and *Essence.com* and all of my editors over there for your support of my work.

And I will close this book (again) the same way I closed every column.

Wishing you all love and ceaseless joy! NHW

www.ingramcontent.com/pod-product-compliance
Lightning Source LLC
LaVergne TN
LVHW051543070426
835507LV00021B/2373